Education for a Beautiful Life

Complicated Conversation

A Book Series of
Curriculam Studies

William F. Pinar.
Series Editor

Volume 63

Christoph Teschers

Education for a Beautiful Life

PETER LANG
New York · Berlin · Bruxelles · Chennai · Lausanne · Oxford

Library of Congress Cataloging-in-Publication Data

Names: Teschers, Christoph, author.
Title: Education for a beautiful life / Christoph Teschers.
Description: New York, NY : Peter Lang, [2025] | Series: Complicated conversation, 1534-2816 ; Volume 63 | Includes bibliographical references and index.
Identifiers: LCCN 2024043591 (print) | LCCN 2024043592 (ebook) | ISBN 9781636671703 (paperback) | ISBN 9781636670775 (pdf) | ISBN 9781636670782 (epub)
Subjects: LCSH: Education—Philosophy. | Schmid, Wilhelm, 1953- Philosophie der Lebenskunst. | Education—Psychological aspects. | Conduct of life.
Classification: LCC LB14.7 .T475 2025 (print) | LCC LB14.7 (ebook) | DDC 370.1—dc23/eng/20241031
LC record available at https://lccn.loc.gov/2024043591
LC ebook record available at https://lccn.loc.gov/2024043592
DOI 10.3726/b22432

Bibliographic information published by the Deutsche Nationalbibliothek. The German National Library lists this publication in the German National Bibliography; detailed bibliographic data is available
on the Internet at http://dnb.d-nb.de.

Cover design by Peter Lang Group AG

ISSN 1534-2816 (print)
ISBN 9781636671703 (paperback)
ISBN 9781636670775 (ebook)
ISBN 9781636670782 (epub)
DOI 10.3726/b22432

© 2025 Peter Lang Group AG, Lausanne
Published by Peter Lang Publishing Inc., New York, USA
info@peterlang.com - www.peterlang.com

All rights reserved.
All parts of this publication are protected by copyright.
Any utilization outside the strict limits of the copyright law, without the permission of the publisher, is forbidden and liable to prosecution.
This applies in particular to reproductions, translations, microfilming, and storage and processing in electronic retrieval systems.

This publication has been peer reviewed.

For my mum and dad, Monika and Winfried Teschers

CONTENTS

Acknowledgements	ix
Introduction	xi

Chapter 1. The Challenge of Living a 'Beautiful Life' in a Changing World — 1

Chapter 2. Wellbeing and Happiness in Contemporary Education — 15

Chapter 3. The Art of Living for Individual and Community Good — 31

Chapter 4. Equity and 'Equal Educational Opportunity' for a Beautiful Life — 59

Chapter 5. The Art of Living as an End of Education — 79

Chapter 6. Education for an Art of Living — 97

Chapter 7. Concluding Thoughts – Good Education in a Changing World 117

Credits 123
Index 125

ACKNOWLEDGEMENTS

As with many larger undertakings, such as writing a book such as this, it is not really the work of one but the work of many that have contributed in various ways to bring this book to life. The most immediate people who have supported my work (and had to contend with me being somewhat preoccupied with it at times) are my wife Barbara and my two children Niklas and Daniella. Thank you for your support and love.

I would also like to thank series Editor William Pinar for accepting my proposal into the *Critical Conversations* book series, and the reviewers of the initial proposal and the final manuscript for their careful read and constructive feedback. Further, my heartfelt thanks go to several colleagues and critical friends, who have supported me by providing considered feedback on early chapter drafts: Laura D'Olimpio, Michael Hand, Michael-John Turp, Claudia Rozas-Gómes, and Peter Roberts. I would also like to thank the Peter Lang publishing team, including Alison Jefferson and Joshua Charles, for their kind support during the writing and publishing process. It has been a pleasure working with you.

Further, I want to acknowledge colleagues who have supported my research work and thinking over the years. My thanks to Maria Nieto for our collaborative work on indigenous approaches to the art of living, particularly in Colombia and the South Americas, which is has informed Chapter Three. My thanks also go to Te Hurinui Clarke, with whom I continue to explore indigenous Māori approaches to an art of living in Aotearoa New Zealand, which informed the sections on indigenous worldviews and education across various chapters. Laura D'Olimpio and I have published on the relation between Philosophy for Children and the art of living, which, among others, informed parts of Chapter Six. And Michaela Vogt and Till Neuhaus have worked with me on the art of living and education from a German cultural perspective, which particularly informed Chapters Six and Seven.

Having reached the mid-point of my career, it seems timely to also thank some of the key influencing figures that helped shape my thinking and academic endeavours. Jörg Zirfas first introduced me during my postgraduate studies in Germany to the philosophy of the art of living, which became a key focus of my work. Peter Roberts has been my PhD supervisor at the time and a mentor for me for many years. I would further like to acknowledge Wilhelm Schmid as key philosopher whose work has shaped my thinking and work fundamentally. I also found Gert Biesta's writing inspiring and his many books and articles have strongly influenced my own understanding of education. A final thanks has to go to all the many people and colleagues that have inspired me through their articles, conference presentations, personal conversations, and email exchanges.

INTRODUCTION

This book is written during a time of relative uncertainty about the future of peace and conflict in parts of the world, such as Ukraine, Eastern Europe, and Russia, as well as in the Middle East, due to the conflict in Gaza and Israel. Recent events, including the global COVID-19 pandemic, the war in Afghanistan, the conflict in Syria, and other localised conflicts and food insecurity have led to mass migration and displacement of people in many parts of the world. The political landscape has also seen a shift over the past decade, with a rise of populist, nationalist parties and politicians challenging not only globalisation but democratic processes and democracy itself in several countries.

Beyond the global and political challenges of our time, education systems, schools, centres, and teachers seem constantly confronted by demands for change due to, for example, international comparative testing such as PISA or the TIMMS study, or national challenges due to change of governments leading to a changing landscape of policy and top-down ministerial directives[1].

---

1 For example, in New Zealand, where this book is written, the education sector, over the past six years, has seen a massive consultation process and overhaul of the national curriculum, assessment and reporting requirements, changes to conditions of teacher practice, and after the recent change in government, a re-introduction of a semi-private schooling system, parallel to state schools, in form of charter schools.

Educators and schools are also often blamed for the effect of wider challenges in societies and called upon to make changes on a wider social level. As such, calls for schools to 'fix inequality', 'fix the loss of social values and norms', or just 'fix the young' reappear again and again every couple of years in many societies. I have encountered messages like these in the media and public debate repeatedly while living in Germany in the 1990s and early 2000s. In New Zealand, where I reside now, just recently schools and teachers have been called upon by the government to 'fix' the decline in reading achievement of New Zealand students through a new mandated literacy programme (i.e., a call for change in what teachers do in schools), even though recent research and reports indicate that only 16.5% of variance in reading achievement is due to school factors and the main challenge and influencing factors lie outside of schools' sphere of influence, such as the socio-economic context of students, their peers, and other individual factors (Hughson & Hood, 2022; Curtis, Nielsen and Derby, 2024).

As a backdrop of these local and global challenges in society and education, we must draw attention again to the questions of what education and schooling are actually *for* (cf. Biesta, 2022) and what they can and cannot do (cf. Bowles & Gintis, 2002). However, we should also – to turn the common question on its head – ask what society *should do for education* (cf. Liebau, 1999). For educators, the question then arises, what is their role in supporting their students to navigate this challenging and changing world? These questions form the basis for the complicated conversations I offer in this book to explore what education *is* or *should be* for, what it *can* and *should* do, and how current expectations placed on education in terms of, for example, student wellbeing and calls for equity in society, can be considered. Following Liebau's reversed question, and considering the constraints of the national and cultural context schools find themselves in (Bowles & Gintis, 2002), I also comment on what our societies should do for education and for our young generation to support them in these changing times. To address these complicated conversations, this book offers seven chapters that address various aspects of these matters which can be read in isolation, but also build on each other to make a larger point for a change in how we can and should consider and *practice* 'good education' (cf. Biesta, 2022).

In Chapter One, I ask the question of how we can live a good and maybe 'beautiful life' in our changing world. Here, I expand on the challenges and current developments, reflecting on how developments in life have sped up and evolved over the last 50-odd years and what that might mean for people and education. I introduce Schmid's (2000a) concept of the art of living as a possible answer in this context, which sets the scene for the rest of the book. I explore how Schmid's art of living can contribute to addressing the different challenges posed for education, schools, centres, and teachers.

One of the current challenges in education that has seen increasing attention in recent years is the question of the wellbeing and happiness of students in education. In Chapter Two, I offer a critique of the term and varied conceptual understandings of 'wellbeing' and 'student wellbeing' and offer Schmid's understanding of a 'beautiful life' as a more holistic and more appropriate approach in place of the rather narrow understanding of 'wellbeing' as the absence of physical, mental, or emotional distress. I also draw attention to the distinction of 'wellbeing *in* education' and 'wellbeing *through* education'. The latter, I position as a more forward-facing consideration that, I argue, might be hindered by a narrower understanding of 'wellbeing' only considered as 'in education' or 'in schools'.

Expanding on the wellbeing theme, in Chapter Three, I turn to the wider challenge of how education should not only support the wellbeing and 'good' of the individual but also the 'good' of the community and society. Here, I consider Schmid's *ethics of the art of living* in conjunction with selected indigenous worldviews and approaches to community good, to discuss how an education for the art of living can not only support the development of students' beautiful lives but also contribute to the wider 'good' for community, society, humanity, and the planet as our living environment.

Chapter Four then continues the theme of individual and society good by considering the question of *equity in education* and *equal educational opportunities*. This chapter is presented in two parts: Part 1 provides a summary of key themes and contentions of the equity debate in education. Part 2 offers a slightly different outlook on equity and equal educational opportunities through the lens of the art of living. While no final answers can be offered here to resolve this complicated matter, I hope that the arguments presented might help to consider a possible way forward towards more equity *in* education but also *through* education for students and societies.

In Chapter Five, I bring the first key line of argument in the book to a point, calling for Schmid's art of living to be an end, if not *the* end, of education. A summary of my previous argument in this context is offered as a starting point, which I then expand in considering how Schmid's art of living as an end of education resonates with selected other positions in the education debate, including Biesta's (2022) *World-centred education*, and the notion of flourishing as an aim of education (e.g., Kristjánsson, 2019).

Having established the key notion that education is, or should be, inherently about the development of students' own art of living, I explore in Chapter Six how such an education could look in practice and how it relates to competency-based approaches to education, as dominant in the United States (US), United Kingdom (UK), and other English-speaking contexts. Drawing on alternative approaches, such as the German (and, e.g., Finnish) notion of *Bildung*, as well as Pinar's (2011) *currere*, I offer considerations how education and schooling could be considered differently. Among others, curriculum themes as well as pedagogical considerations for teaching practice are included here as well.

The book closes with the final Chapter Seven, returning to the challenge of how to enact 'good education' in a changing world. This chapter is written particularly with educators in mind, offering a call to action from the bottom up rather than waiting for change from the top down, which Bowles and Gintis (2002) and Tyack and Tobin (1994) have argued is slow to come (if at all). Our changing world is now, and our students need to be prepared for a future world that is nearly impossible for us to predict today. So, we need to find ways of *doing* education that will support them to find their way through this changing world.

References

Hughson, T., & Hood, N. (2022). What's happening with literacy in Aotearoa New Zealand? https://www.theeducationhub.org.nz

Curtis, D., Nielsen, P., & Derby, M. (2024, May 16). Reframing the reading debate: a path to equity and excellence – Ipu Kererū. Ipu Kererū. https://nzareblog.wordpress.com/2024/05/16/reframing-the-reading-debate/

· 1 ·
THE CHALLENGE OF LIVING A 'BEAUTIFUL LIFE' IN A CHANGING WORLD

What does it mean to live a good or beautiful life? This question will emerge for most people at some point in their life – likely more than once. In history, many answers have been suggested; however, arguably there is no one single answer, as any response is always contextual, temporal and, yes, individual. That does not mean, however, that we cannot offer support for people to find these answers for themselves in their social, cultural and temporal context. One concept that can help people navigate their way through the jungle of possibilities is Wilhelm Schmid's (2000) *Philosophie der Lebenskunst* [philosophy of the art of living], which I will introduce in more detail later in this chapter and discuss throughout the book. Before I come to this, it seems relevant to outline some of the larger complexities of people's lives today and the resulting challenges for figuring out how living a good life might look like. While it is not my intend to depress the reader by listing what amounts to significant challenges of our time, it is of particular importance in the context of education, as I would argue that current approaches to education and schooling in many countries are not equipping our young generation well to deal with these complexities of life and to find their own answers to this key question.

Challenges for People's Life Today

As indicated in the Introduction, this book is written at the tail end of the Covid-19 pandemic in the early 2020s, which has placed a lot of constrictions and challenges on people's lives. The pandemic is one example of the complexities of our globalised world in the twenty-first century. As another example, cultural diversity in our increasingly multi-cultural societies could be named. This is not to say that multiculturism is to be avoided, but rather that globalisation presents the opportunity for global movement which creates the challenges of having to choose a place and country to live in, as well as being confronted with different cultural values, norms, beliefs, and practices more often today than has been common for past generations. As such, the excessive increase in choices for life in principle, but also daily, forms one of the key challenges, I would argue, for people today. Barry Schwartz (2004), for example, explains in his book *The Paradox of Choice* that human beings are easily overwhelmed when offered more than a handful of options for a single decision. According to Schwartz, this can have various implications, including keeping people from making a choice in the first place – i.e., the paradox of effectively losing the freedom of choice by not being able to make a decision due to its complexity. Another consequence can be increasing levels of mental fatigue as exploring available options sufficiently to make a satisfactory decision requires significantly more mental energy than having only a handful of options to consider. This increase in options and opportunities, I claim, extends to most if not all areas of life, such as the aforementioned question of where to live (not just regional, or national, but globally), the decision of what one wants to do for work – children and young people today are often told they 'can be whatever they want to be', which includes hundreds if not thousands of possible professions; how can one make a reasonably informed choice under these circumstances? Another area is the question of how to fill one's time: competing offers of what we should spend our 'free time' on have increased significantly since the end of the twentieth century. Similarly, our choice of products in any single category has exploded, may it be the uncountable options of smartphones on the marked, or (using a personal example) the incredible number of options of tinned tuna in the grocery store. Schwartz explains in this context that making satisfactory choices, which are choices we feel good about, becomes more difficult as we always have to ask ourselves if, with all these options, we could not have found a product or made a choice that is even better for our context. And while some of the criteria for choosing might predominantly be personal preference, such as taste (tuna) or functionality (smartphone), considering today's environmental crises as well as the issue of modern slavery, ethical criteria may and should also play a role in our decision making as well. This again adds another layer of complexity to evaluating each option. These ethical questions, however, of 'what is the right thing to do' or the 'right action' in any given situation have also become more challenging due to competing values that are presented to us in societies today through family, peers, culture, and media, and are further diversified through our globalised world. In fact, one of the key aspects of Schmid's art of living approach is the ability (and requirement) to reflect on the norms, values, and beliefs one is presented with and to make conscious decisions about which of these one wants to actively subscribe to and align one's life choices and actions with accordingly.

A final example I want to offer regarding the complexities of life, which is likely only to increase in future, is the rapid developments in technology and the accompanying changes for our daily life and work. Computers and the Internet, including social media, have arguably been the most disruptive developments in this century so far, followed by, maybe more subtle, online shopping and delivery which is rapidly changing the landscape of how we shop. Further significant changes are on the horizon, with self-driving cars, flying modes of transportation, work from home arrangements (sped up by the recent global pandemic), artificial intelligence, and medical advancements that might be able to prolong life significantly beyond what is currently considered the average life expectancy. All these developments can impact significantly on how people live, what they value, and how work is structured. These historically fairly rapid changes impact on our daily life, and so people's views on how a good life might look like might change more rapidly over time as well. These challenges outlined above also create issues for people's mental health and wellbeing, which, according to the World Health Organisation (WHO, 2022), is an ongoing and increasing problem today, which is not helped by current cultural and social expectations surrounding happiness and wellbeing as they are portrayed in the media and exasperated through social media. I will discuss some of the issues of wellbeing and happiness in relation to education in Chapter Two.

Different Cultures and Worldviews

Moving beyond these somewhat common and shared challenges of our time, I will now comment briefly on cultural messaging and memes (cf. Isaacs, 2020). As I am residing in Aotearoa New Zealand at the time of writing this book, drawing on so-called 'Western' and 'Indigenous' worldviews, and in relation to the latter particularly the Māori worldview (as far as I can understand it, being conscious of my white European heritage), seems appropriate in this context. I want to point out first, however, that it is not my intent to juxtapose two different cultural perspectives, but rather to reflect on dominant views and values that seem to permeate 'Western' countries through a different approach to life and seeing the world. It needs to be said that any portrayal of Indigenous values here is based on my understanding at this point in time, based on the engagement I had with individuals and the reading I have done in this context, and will undoubtedly fall short of the complexity and nuances each of the concepts and values presented below represent. Similarly, there is neither a singular Indigenous nor a singular 'Western', or Asian or any other homogenous kind of worldview. However, there might be some shared understandings and values that lead to these categories being used and I will indicate some of these here. I would also like to draw attention to Biesta's (2023) considerations surrounding the aspect of perspectivism and his questioning if approaching cultural encounters through this lens being helpful – which he suggests it is not. Biesta rather argues that encounters with others should not default to categorising (and reducing) individuals as agents of a culture, which 'runs the risk of replacing this encounter itself with an explanation of the encounter' and placing 'the other at a safe distance from me' (p. 248). For Biesta, the more pertinent question is not how to perceive the Other as other, but what does this encounter ask of *me*? In this spirit, I approach the engagement with cultural worldviews or narratives not as framing or categorising them nor to create juxtapositions but in trying to be open to the transformational possibilities that these encounters might present.

To start with the familiar, one shared context of what is often referred to as 'Western' societies (i.e., central Europe, North Amerika, but also Australia and New Zealand), for example, is the dominant ideology of neoliberalism, including aspects such as a focus on the individual and individual choice, marketization of not only the economy but most aspects of society, a strive to performativity and an obsession with accountability. This has significant impact on our societies, (young) people's worldviews and wellbeing, as well as our education systems and views on education (cf. Roberts & Peters, 2008; Roberts & Codd, 2010; Nairn, Sligo & Higgins, 2012; Biesta, 2015). Some of the consequences that can be seen following this ideology is a cultural norm of competitiveness – phrases like 'one needs to get ahead' or 'to get a leg up' are indicative of this – as well as a tendency to consumerism, fuelled by the false cultural belief and the messaging of a global marketing industry that 'having more' leads to more happiness in life (cf. Layard, 2011). However, despite some of the challenging ideology that impacts much of 'Western' societies, other shared values (in some countries, and by some held more strongly than others) are freedom (of choice), social justice, equity, democratic processes, and basic human rights. One could argue that underlying these values is an aspect of care, care for the people and care for society, to flourish, express themselves and live a 'good life' (however that is defined in the respective context). One could further argue that these latter values are in conflict with the messaging that permeates many societies around competition, consumerism and a somewhat narcissist view of self-centred egoism. And in fact, it seems to me that human interaction on a personal level and in relationships with friends and family is much more guided by values of care and reciprocal support than by competition. The latter seems to creep in more in environments where people feel a level of separation in their relationship to the other, or where the system at play is designed deliberately to encourage competition, such as in some places of work, some social circles and – unfortunately – in schools (cf. Biesta, 2015).

Looking at selected indigenous values and worldviews – again, being aware of its somewhat stereotypical generalisation – this underlying aspect of care seems stronger in focus and more dominant in the values and practices that guide human interaction. Often referred to values in the Māori context in Aotearoa New Zealand, for example, include *manaakitanga* [care and hospitality], *kotahitanga* [unity], *whanaungatanga* [relationships] and *whakapapa* [genealogy], to name only some[1]. I would argue that it is not too far off the mark to suggest that *te ao Māori* [Māori worldview] is inherently relational. The values and practices of whanaungatanga and whakapapa focus on establishing relationships between people and relationships to ancestors, land and nature. Manaakitanga and kotahitanga both support caring relationships between people and groups. Manaakitanga, for example, stipulates to care for guests and to uphold and further the *mana* [respect; dignity] of the other. In reciprocity, one's own mana is strengthened if manaakitanga is done well. Kotahitanga, according to Savage et al. (2014), promotes unity and is expressed through enabling voices of all to be heard. As underlying

---

1 The discussion of these values is based on my understanding derived from living and working in Aotearoa New Zealand, including partaking in a number of cultural workshops offered at my university, as well as my reading of many articles discussing these and other values in relation to education and schooling. Examples for the interested reader to start with regarding Māori values in education would be MacFarlane, 2004, Savage et al., 2014, and Macfarlane & Macfarlane, 2019. The translations offered here are common, but do not capture all layers of meaning of the original Māori terms.

values or principles to guide all action in Māoridom, *tika* [right; correct], *pono* [integrity; fairness] and *aroha* [care; compassion] are often named (Savage et al., 2014). One can see, I would argue, connections between these values and the underlying values of care that can be seen in 'Western' cultural contexts, as suggested above. However, one significant distinction stands out in this context: the aspect of care and relationship in Māoridom extends to nature and our planet. In te ao Māori, humans are not the owners of our environment, inherited from our ancestors (which seems to be a common belief in non-indigenous, predominantly 'Western' societies), but we are the custodians to look after the environment for our children and our children's children. Another inherent difference, which is often mentioned in Western-Indigenous discussions, is the focus on the community in indigenous cultures rather than on the individual as in our westernised world. Most, if not all, aspects of life seem to be considered from a community perspective, or even from a position of community identity, which can be difficult to understand for people socialised in Western cultural contexts. Similarly difficult to grasp is the notion of our planet earth and nature as an entity that deserves respect and has rights like a 'real' person. Nevertheless, examples exist where aspects of nature have been granted 'personhood' and associated rights in countries largely based on Western legal frameworks. Examples are the Whanganui river in the North Island of Aotearoa New Zealand (NZ Parliament, 2017) and the Ganges river in India (Tanasescu, 2017). In a recent article on this topic, Putzer et al. (2022) identified 409 initiatives across 39 countries that aim to grant legal rights to parts of nature. As such, we can already see a strong influence of indigenous worldviews on governments and societies. Similarly influential, I would argue, can be to reflect on the cultural memes – the messages we, as individuals, receive and are given by our local culture. These include messages, like the focus on personal benefit and gain rather than seeing one's place as part of a community and society, of ownership over nature and land rather than stewardship and care for our environment for future generations, and the idea that personal standing might come from the care one gives others, to name only a few examples. To engage in such reflection on some of the fundamental and often sub-conscious messages that form our worldview requires certain skills, awareness, openness, knowledge and understanding, however. Which is where we enter the field of education. What are the skills, knowledge areas, and understanding to help us to reflect on and potentially change the fundamentals of what forms our identity? How can awareness for key issues be gained and maintained? What is necessary for students 'to stay with what they encounter . . . , so that they can figure out what the world may be asking of them' (Biesta, 2023: 249)? Some answers to these questions are suggested in Schmid's (2000) philosophy of the art of living, which I will turn to now.

Schmid's Concept of the Art of Living

Wilhelm Schmid, a contemporary German philosopher, has developed a philosophical approach towards an art of living and what can be said about living a good life – or, as he calls it, a beautiful life [*schönes Leben*]. Schmid deliberately chooses the term 'beautiful' as he argues that the term 'good life' is laden with pre-conceived cultural ideas about what it means and looks like. Fred Feldman (2004), similarly, points out that a 'good life' can be understood in different ways: morally good (a good person), biologically good (in line with evolutionary concepts), financially good (amassing wealth and amenities), or hedonistic good (a life of pleasures and happiness). Schmid argues, however, that approaches to what it might mean to live a good life are likely diverse as there are people alive. Therefore, we cannot prescribe from the outside how a 'good life' might look like and how each person should be living. Consequently, Schmid (2000) chooses the term *beautiful life* to express that the judgement about one's life lies in the eyes of the person living it. Like a work of art, beauty cannot be defined but lies in the eyes of the beholder. Similarly, a painting, for example, might be judged by some as beautiful and simultaneously dismissed by others. To live a beautiful life, however, is not a matter of luck or happenstance. Schmid argues that it takes care and deliberate action to shape one's own life into what one might perceive a beautiful life to be. One must become the artist who shapes one's own life into a piece of art through engaging in what he calls: the art of living[2].

To engage in the art of living, for Schmid, means to take responsibility for one's own life; not to be driven by external expectations but to reflect on what is important for oneself and taking deliberate action to shape one's life

---

2 Schmid uses the German term *Lebenskunst* [art of living], which is somewhat common in German language and has different connotations, but largely refers to someone who is able to navigate life well and enjoys life with all its ups and downs. It is often used to describe people who follow a somewhat different lifestyle from the norm, i.e., people who create or shape their own life based on their own norms, values and beliefs.

accordingly. It means to not mindlessly accept the values, norms and beliefs (the memes, so to speak) of one's family, society and culture, but to reflect actively on which of the beliefs and values one is presented with align with who one wants to be and how one wants to live one's life. Therefore, to engage in the art of living requires care and labour[3]. It is not something that will happen by itself but requires regular reflection – not only on one's values and beliefs but also on one's actions. We must ask ourselves, is what I am doing in line with what I value, who I want to be and how I want to live my life? To illustrate, I will consider two examples.

As first example, I want to reflect on one of the underlying beliefs in many Western societies that suggests that everyone has a fair chance and that one's ability and effort define one's standing in society. This meritocratic idea underpinning neoliberal ideology is widespread and not well reflected in people's daily life. It underpins views of and in society that stigmatise the poor, or the 'underachiever', as either lazy or as not capable. It also leads to significant pressures on particularly young people who internalise (academic) underachievement with personal failure rather than to consider the wider personal and societal circumstances that make a significant different for a student's ability to achieve. Circumstances such as socio-economic status, educational background of the parents, social and other forms of capital (see Bourdieu), cultural fit between student and teacher and a host of other aspects (see, for example, Keddie, 2016) play a significant role for a student's success but lie outside of their control. This concept of meritocracy has been debunked as a myth some time ago (e.g., McNamee & Miller, 2004); however, it still remains as an underlying cultural belief in many societies and is as such suggested to (young) people living in societies today. A person engaged in the art of living will have to question this belief and reflect on the wider societal circumstances that constrain a person's ability to reach certain levels in society (or education) based on their starting position in society and their personal circumstances (e.g., are they looking after dependent relatives, do they have to support their family from an early age, are aspects of discrimination playing a role, etc.). This person will come to understand the flawed nature of this belief and will have to adjust their own set of beliefs and worldview, followed by a reflection on their actions. For example, if a teacher did belief that success in school (and society) is based on personal ability and effort of a student, they

---

3   Schmid draws on Foucault's (1984) *Care of the self* and his concept of the 'labour of care' in this context.

will have to change this belief and act accordingly. This would include to take into consideration the family situation as well as the wider social and cultural aspects that influence this student's ability to achieve in the classroom and find ways to support the student to succeed rather than to leave the burden on the student alone.

Another example would be the labour of adjusting one's actions in line with one's values. If we, for example, would value the continued existence of humanity, and belief in generational fairness of allowing future generations to grow up and live in an environment that remains similarly supportive of human life on our planet as what we are allowed to experience, we will come to believe in the value of sustainability and the protection of our natural environment. Subscribing to this view is not enough, however: we would then have to reflect on our actions in our daily life and consider what actions may have particular impact on our environmental footprint. This might start with the holidays we have planned, our method of travel and the impact of our trip on the local environment, but it also extends into our daily life in other ways, such as which products we buy in the supermarket, where they are sourced, how environmentally friendly they are produced, and so on. Some of these aspects and consequences of our actions on the environment will be quite obvious; for others, we need to be able to see the interconnections of actions, reactions and consequences on a larger scale in our globalised world, which requires further skills such as critical thinking, prudence and practical wisdom.

These examples show how an engagement in the art of living requires us, as Schmid argues, to reflect on the norms, values, and beliefs that guide our life, who we want to be, as well as our actions. They also presuppose, however, certain values of justice and fairness. A common argument brought forth in response to the individual nature in Schmid's approach to the art of living and what it might mean to live a beautiful life, however, is the question of what happens if one's values and pursuit of a 'beautiful life' might impact on other people's freedom and ability to do the same? A response to this challenge lies in Schmid's (2000) ethical model that is based on, what he calls, the *enlightened self-interest* of the individual. Schmid argues that in our post-modern individualistic societies, external entities for providing moral values – such as religion, churches but also governments – have lost and are losing authority and validity. Therefore, he developed an *ethics model* for the art of living that is based on the self-interest of the individual rather than any external entity, arguing that self-interest is an inherent motivation for people to act. Schmid draws then on Aristotle's (1996) notion of *phronésis* [prudence; practical wisdom] as a key aspect of engaging in the art of living. Through prudence and practical wisdom, he argues, one will come to understand that one has a higher chance of living a beautiful life if the environment one is living in is supportive of such aspirations and the development of their own art of living. So, as a member of a society (as most people are), it is advisable to create an environment that is conducive for each person to develop their own art of living. Hence, one's own version of a beautiful life should not impact on the ability of other people to develop their own art of living and pursuit of a beautiful life. Prudence will further lead to the realisation that, if one unduly impacts on the rights and freedom of others in a society, consequences will be imposed on the one overstepping the boundaries and as such one's ability to live what one sees a beautiful life to be, will be impacted. As I have discussed Schmid's ethics model in more detail in a previous publication (Teschers, 2018), I will contend to state here that through *phronésis*, basic self-interest – egoism, one could say – will be transformed into a form of enlightened self-interest that leads to an ethical model of care: the care for the self, the care for others, the care for society and humanity, and the care for the environment and our planet. I will revisit this concept in more detail in Chapter Three.

The Role of Education for the Art of Living

Having introduced Schmid's concept of the art of living above, I will now briefly discuss the role education can play for the development of students' (and other people's) art of living. Throughout the book, it will become apparent that I argue for the existence of a reciprocal relationship between the art of living and education; however, I will focus on the one direction of this relationship in this chapter and will discuss the relevance of the art of living for education and resulting implications in more detail in the later chapters of this book.

In the section above, some key abilities or faculties for the development of an art of living have been mentioned, including (self-) reflection, *phronésis* [prudence and practical wisdom][4], critical thinking, and the ability to see the interconnections in the world. Schmid emphasises the importance of the

---

4 Embedded in these is the not unproblematic assumption of the ability to rational thought. While much could be said about rationality of human beings (or the lack thereof), at this point the ability to learn to understand basic causality and logic shall be deemed as fundamental abilities for the development of an art of living.

latter for the art of living and the ability to shape one's life actively. Without being able to see the interconnections [Zusammenhänge] in the world, one cannot take targeted actions to effect change and would rather stumble blindly through life, so to speak. As discussed elsewhere (Teschers et al., 2024), these interconnections in the world, Schmid refers to, can be any kind of causal relations, starting from simply physical cause-effect relationships (such as being able to turn on the light by flicking the light switch), to social relationships (for example, understanding the importance of social, cultural and symbolic capital (cf. Bourdieu, 2013) to open doors and opportunities in society), to societal relations on a global scale (such as understanding how unchecked consumerism, and one's personal responsibility for the choices one makes, in one country can contribute to the exploitation of slave-like workers in another). Only by being able to understand how one's actions in one context 'ripple out' in consequences for people in other contexts, one can make conscious decisions to act in accordance with one's values, norms, and beliefs. To be able to understand these interconnections, one needs to gain not just the ability of critical thinking to dissect relationships and causalities, but one also needs to have a fairly broad knowledge base and understanding of the world one is living in, what could be considered *Bildung* in German language and loosely translates as formation and culturation of human beings: being knowledgeable about the world and possessing prudence and practical wisdom to act appropriately in one's daily context[5].

Here we have arrived at the role education can have for the art of living: equipping students to gain the necessary knowledge and understanding, relevant to their local and personal context, and the necessary skills and faculties (such as thinking skills, prudence and practical wisdom, (self-)reflection) to be able to develop their own art of living under the circumstances they are living in. I will expand on this point in more detail in Chapters Five and Six of this book.

---

5   While this is a somewhat idealised understanding of *Bildung*, a term which has different connotations depending on the context it is used in German and English literature, it is used here to suggest a combination of certain knowledge areas, understanding and faculties (such as critical thinking, prudence and practical wisdom) as foundation to action purposeful and effective change. The details of what knowledge and understanding is necessary to do so, however, depends on the circumstances and context one is living in. It will be quite different for someone living in central Europe to someone living in the Middle East, Asia, or for members of indigenous communities in different parts of the world.

Conclusion

In this chapter, I have argued that we are living in a changing world. A world that is progressing more quickly in many ways than it has for the lived experience of human beings in our history so far. It is also likely, considering the recent advancements in technology, communication, artificial intelligence, medicine, and other areas, that changes for current and future generations will become even more fast paced than we have experienced so far. As such, we are challenged not only with the need 'to keep up' with the developments in our lives and work environments but also with an increasing number of options for any given choice we make. When writing this book, serious efforts are under way to establish the first permanent base on the moon and a first human presence on Mars in the coming fifteen to twenty years, which suggests that the grandchildren of my generation might not only have to decide where they want to live on our planet, but if they maybe want to live somewhere else entirely. However, staying closer to home, I have discussed the broadening range of worldviews and cultural norms people today are exposed to in many if not most countries through globalisation and migration. I also suggested that the often-proclaimed divide between so-called 'Western' and Indigenous knowledges and worldviews might have connecting points that allow us to reflect on our own personal and cultural perspective through other lenses. I would argue that such reflection would be particularly helpful in combating some of the more harmful excesses neoliberal ideology has brought into (Western) ways of thinking. Finally, I introduced Schmid's philosophical concept of the art of living and argued that education can play a significant role to develop the knowledge areas, skills and faculties necessary for people to develop their own art of living and shape their lives actively into what they might perceive a beautiful life to be. In the following chapters, I will expand on most of the themes and concepts introduced here as indicated above.

References

Aristotle. (1996). *The Nicomachean ethics*. Edited by T. Griffith. London, England: Wordsworth Editions Limited.

Biesta, G. (2023). 'Becoming contemporaneous: Intercultural communication pedagogy beyond culture and without ethics'. *Pedagogy, Culture & Society, 31*(2), 237–251. doi:10.1080/14681366.2022.2164341.

Biesta, G. J. J. (2015). *Good education in an age of measurement: Ethics, politics, democracy, Good Education in an Age of Measurement: Ethics, Politics, Democracy*. doi:10.4324/9781315634319.

Bourdieu, P. (2013). *Distinction*. Routledge. doi:10.4324/9780203720790.

Feldman, F. (2004). *Pleasure and the good life: Concerning the nature, varieties and plausibility of hedonism*. New York, NY: Clarendon.

Foucault, M. (1984). *The care of the self*. London, England: Penguin Books (The history of sexuality).

Isaacs, D. (2020). 'Memes'. *Journal of Paediatrics and Child Health*, 56(4), 497–498. doi:10.1111/jpc.14755.

Keddie, A. (2016). 'Children of the market: Performativity, neoliberal responsibilisation and the construction of student identities'. *Oxford Review of Education*, 42(1), 108–122. doi:10.1080/03054985.2016.1142865.

Layard, R. (2011). *Happiness: Lessons from a new science*. London, England: Penguin Books.

MacFarlane, A. (2004). *Kia hiwa ra! Listen to culture – Māori students' plea to educators*. Wellington, New Zealand: NZCER.

Macfarlane, A., & Macfarlane, S. (2019). 'Listen to culture: Māori scholars' plea to researchers'. *Journal of the Royal Society of New Zealand*, 49(sup 1), 48–57. doi:10.1080/03036758.2019.1661855.

McNamee, S. J., & Miller, R. K. (2004). 'The meritocracy myth'. *Sociation Today*, 2(1).

Nairn, K. M., Sligo, J., & Higgins, J. (2012). *Children of Rogernomics : A neoliberal generation leaves school*. Dunedin, N.Z.: Otago University Press.

NZ Parliament. (2017). *Innovative bill protects Whanganui River with legal personhood – New Zealand Parliament*. Available at: https://www.parliament.nz/en/get-involved/features/innovative-bill-protects-whanganui-river-with-legal-personhood/ (Accessed: 19 January 2023).

Putzer, A. et al. (2022). 'Putting the rights of nature on the map. A quantitative analysis of rights of nature initiatives across the world'. *Journal of Maps* [Preprint]. doi:10.1080/17445647.2022.2079432/SUPPL_FILE/TJOM_A_2079432_SM1337.PDF.

Roberts, P., & Codd, J. (2010). 'Neoliberal tertiary education policy'. In M. Thrupp & R. Irwin (Eds.), *Another decade of [N]ew [Z]ealand education policy: [W]here to now?* Hamilton, New Zealand: Wilf Malcolm Institute of Educational research, 99–110.

Roberts, P., & Peters, M. A. (2008). *Neoliberalism, higher education and research*. Rotterdam, Netherlands: Sense Publishers.

Savage, C. et al. (2014). 'Huakina mai: A kaupapa Māori approach to relationship and behaviour support'. *Australian Journal of Indigenous Education*, 43(2), 165–174. doi:10.1017/jie.2014.23.

Schmid, W. (2000). *Philosophie der Lebenskunst: Eine Grundlegung*. Frankfurt: Suhrkamp.

Schwartz, B. (2004). *The paradox of choice: Why more is less*. New York, NY: ECCO.

Tanasescu, M. (2017). 'When a river is a person: From Ecuador to New Zealand, nature gets its day in court'. *Open Rivers Rethinking Water Place & Community*, 8, 127–132. doi:10.24926/2471190X.3300.

Teschers, C. (2018). *Education and Schmid's Art of Living, Education and Schmid's Art of Living*. Routledge. doi:10.4324/9781315563848.

Teschers, C., Neuhaus, T., & Vogt, M. (2024). Troubling the boundaries of traditional schooling for a rapidly changing future – Looking back and looking forward. *Educational Philosophy and Theory*, (early online), 1–12. doi:10.1080/00131857.2024.2321932.

WHO. (2022). *Transforming mental health for all*. BMJ. doi:10.1136/bmj.o1593.

· 2 ·

WELLBEING AND HAPPINESS IN CONTEMPORARY EDUCATION

I argue in this chapter that wellbeing is often understood in a limited way and that a more holistic approach is needed, if we want to address personal and societal challenges people and humanity face today and in the future. The philosophical concept of the art of living will be employed as a lens that can support people to live a 'beautiful life' in a holistic approach to wellbeing. Ethical and practical implications for society and education will be discussed and an argument made for a shift in educational focus towards an education for the art of living to support people's personal well-lived and beautiful life. This might potentially also support a shift in society that can promote more equity and fairness for people to develop their own art of living and live a beautiful life, which will be discussed further in Chapter Three.

Troubling the Notions of Wellbeing and Happiness in Educational Contexts

While the notion of wellbeing has received increased attention in the public and academic discourse in principle and in relation to education and schooling specifically in recent years, it remains contested in meaning and scope[1].

---

1 See Vidal and O'Steen (2023) for a more detailed overview of the notion of *wellbeing* and how it is understood in different contexts and disciplinary traditions.

Notions of wellbeing reach from a rather limited focus on physical and mental health to somewhat more holistic approaches that may include emotional, social/relational, and sometimes spiritual dimensions. However, even broader understandings of wellbeing are still often concerned with people's current state of emotions and recent-past experiences and mostly exclude future focused perspectives of life-trajectories, which I would argue are essential for educational considerations of wellbeing. In contrast, concepts such as *life-satisfaction* and *flourishing* seem to take a longer, even *life-long* perspective[2]. In this context, life-satisfaction seems to be pointed backwards, reflecting on one's life up to this point, whereas flourishing seems to mostly be pointing from the present into the future (e.g., Seligman, 2011; Kristjánsson, 2019). This said, the so-called subjective wellbeing (SWB) concept, often used in positive psychology, draws heavily on life-satisfaction accounts (Kristjánsson, 2019). While there are varying definitions of SWB, it is often understood as some function of one's personal view of satisfaction with one's life at a certain point in time, and the sum of positive emotions and pleasures minus the negative emotions that are salient to individuals at the time of being asked to comment on their SWB (cf. Busseri & Sadava, 2011). In this context, the life-satisfaction account seems to be closely related to the emotional state of the individual, i.e., judgements about how satisfied one is with one's life are influenced by how one feels emotionally at the time of making such judgements. As such, the reference timeframe seemingly depends on what the person in question is considering and experiencing at that point in time, which can be assumed to be influenced by experiences of the recent past.

However, in both psychology and philosophy wellbeing has seen a range of definitions. Generally speaking, different accounts of wellbeing draw on two traditions to varying degrees: (i) the *hedonistic* tradition focused on subjective experiences of pleasures and positive emotions linked to the notion of life-satisfaction and subjective wellbeing, and (ii) the Aristotelian-inspired *eudaimonic* tradition focusing more strongly on objective measures of optimal human functioning, more often linked to the notions of *happiness* and, more recently, *flourishing* (cf. Kristjánsson, 2019; Vidal & O'Steen, 2023). For Aristotle (1996), *eudaimonia* is the state of *utmost happiness*, which some describe as an experience of *serene happiness* (Müller-Commichau, 2007, my translation): a state of being that we pursue as an end in itself rather than a

---

2 While from the concepts mentioned here, flourishing resonates most with an art of living approach to education, differences between the concepts exist and will be discussed in Chapter 5. For now, I will focus on the notion of wellbeing in my discussion.

means to any other end. Aristotle (1996) argued that everything we do is aimed towards achieving this state of eudaimonia.

As indicated above, eudaimonia is often translated as 'flourishing' in more recent publications (e.g., Kristjánsson, 2019)[3], and while these two concepts are likely related, I would argue that they are not synonymous. In contrast to Kristjánsson (2019) and Seligman (2011), I would rather see the relationship as one of correlation: if a person is flourishing in life, it is more likely that this person might reach the state of eudaimonia more often than people who are not. I would not, however, go so far as to state a causal relationship nor assume that flourishing would be a necessity for eudaimonia. This would depend strongly on how flourishing is defined, and the term is used somewhat differently, similar to wellbeing and happiness, depending on discipline and context. The challenge for education is that definitions and understandings of this and other concepts are often borrowed from either philosophy or psychology. Over the last decade or so, these lines have blurred as positive psychologists have started to link their work and understanding of flourishing to a form of neo-Aristotelean understanding of eudaimonia in the philosophical tradition (Kristjánsson, 2019). Kristjánsson argues, however, that the account of eudaimonia used in positive psychology literature falls somewhat short of some of the key aspects of Aristotle's argument, especially in relation to the understanding of *virtues* and the ethical and moral aspects of the concept.

When considering these concepts from an educational perspective, further complexities arise. While the definitions of 'wellbeing', 'happiness' and 'flourishing' are often not clearly defined, and existing definitions vary in detail, which provides challenges for practical application of these concepts in educational practice, one has to further ask the question if the current emphasis on 'student wellbeing', which is often seen as the absence of physical, mental and emotional distress (c.f. Sun & Shek, 2014), is desirable in the first place, and what it means for educational practice if this was the case. One aspect that comes to mind is that 'good education'[4] will from time to time unsettle students and challenge them in their norms, values, beliefs and

---

3 In older texts, eudaimonia has been more commonly translated as 'happiness' (e.g. Seligman 2010); however, happiness is a complex and complicated concept to grasp and in its common use, as well as how it was defined in positive psychology by Seligman and others, does not match well with Aristotle's intentions (cf. Seligman 2011; Kristjánsson 2012).

4 I use the term 'good education' here in a holistic sense that goes beyond the common, and problematic I might add, language of 'learning' in schooling contexts and encompasses a balanced approach to, what Gert Biesta (2013, 2022) has termed, the three aspects of

assumptions. The development of aspects such as subjectification[5] (Biesta, 2013), character and agency, one might argue, are strongly supported by such uncomfortable engagements and the challenging of students' personally held values and beliefs. Moving beyond feelings of comfort, others have argued that much educational (in the wider sense of human development) can be found in experiences of suffering and even despair (cf. Roberts, 2016). A limited notion of 'student wellbeing' that focuses mainly on physical and mental aspects of health and the hedonic tradition of positive emotions will fall short of capturing and allowing such educative experiences. This said, no one would seriously argue that students should not be physically and mentally safe in educational settings that have a responsibility of care for the students they serve[6]. However, physical and mental safety is somewhat different from common conceptions of wellbeing as absence of distress. I would further argue that, when taking a life-long perspective of human development, focusing mainly on the immediate mental and emotional state of students towards positive emotions can have a detrimental effect for their long-term wellbeing and life-satisfaction in future as hardships in life are generally unavoidable and a lack of experiencing such hardship in a safe space that supports the development of coping strategies at the same time seems relevant for managing experiences later in life. I would further argue that this is even more impactful on students' ability to flourish and live successful and meaningful lives, as a narrow focus on positive emotions will likely emphasise subjective pleasures over more meaningful pursuits[7] in life.

At this point, it seems relevant to comment on the recent developments in so-called 'positive education', a sub-discipline of positive psychology. Without wanting to delve into a detailed account of the complexities and

---

    subjectification, socialisation and qualification. Education is understood here as the formation of a human being rather than the mere acquisition of subject content.

5 'Subjectification' can be understood as the becoming of a human being as active agent in the world with a sense of self.

6 The responsibility of care emerges, in my view, predominantly out of the compulsory nature of the education system for children and young people that are not deemed adults yet and therefore have limited freedom and autonomy in this context. For other arguments for an ethics of care in education (with larger implications beyond student safety and wellbeing) see, for example, Noddings (2013).

7 In this context, compare the different pathways Seligman (2011) outlines in relation to happiness and flourishing, which Kristjánsson (2019) argues to represent a hierarchy even if Seligman denies the same.

challenges surrounding this latest trend in education[8], I want to make some cautious points here as they relate to the overall emphasis of wellbeing in education. Positive psychology approaches to education have been critiqued as resembling more closely 'depression avoidance classes' than actual 'happiness classes' (Suissa, 2008). Kristjánsson (2012) argued further that it was still unclear at the time if positive education had anything new or worthwhile to offer education that is not already part of other educational theories in practice. Although some time has passed since these early critiques of positive education that at the time was just emerging, more recent accounts remain cautious of the fit between positive psychology concepts, such as Seligman's PERMA model or Deci and Ryan's Self-Determination-Theory, and more holistic perspectives on wellbeing and flourishing (Kristjánsson, 2019: 29). Considering some of the evidence of studies exploring the impact of positive education for students and teachers (White & Murray, 2015; Sandholm et al., 2022), the focus seems to remain on social and emotional learning, such as improvements in positive emotions, increased gratefulness, more positive feelings towards schools and a correlation with higher performance at school overall. And while most studies (not all!) find improvements in these and other areas, the focus of these studies and practices seems to largely remain on an understanding of wellbeing in the hedonic tradition of subjective emotions and affect. So, I concur with Kristjánsson (2019) that the critique voiced a decade ago still remains that positive psychology and positive education is limited in its approach to wellbeing and certainly continues to fall short of any account of 'flourishing' in Aristotle's eudemonic sense. This said, the contribution positive psychology and positive education can have on supporting mental and emotional wellbeing of students, including increasing their positive feelings towards school, should not be dismissed and can certainly help (young) people to develop important social-emotional skills and coping mechanisms to deal with adversity in their current and future lives.

Considering these philosophical and terminological complexities discussed above, the argument I want to make, however, is that from an educational, as well as human and social development perspective, any notion of 'wellbeing' is most relevant when considered more holistically from a life-wide *and* life-long perspective that aims towards the experience of eudaimonia, of 'serene happiness' (Müller-Commichau, 2007) in the Aristotelian sense.

---

8 See Kristjánsson (2012) for a detailed analysis of positive education in relation to educational philosophy and theory.

However, as the term wellbeing can mostly be regarded as somewhat limited in scope the way it is largely understood, and flourishing remains both vague in many cases and somewhat complicated for practical application in more specific accounts (e.g., Kristjánsson, 2019), I would propose that a different terminology would make more sense to be used in the context of education, namely Wilhelm Schmid's (2000) notion of a *beautiful life* as part of his art of living philosophy.

A 'Beautiful Life' as a Holistic Approach to Wellbeing

As explained in Chapter One, for Schmid, a beautiful life lies in the eye of the person living said life. Like a work of art, beauty lies in the eye of the beholder, and therefore we cannot pre-define how a beautiful life should look like; there are likely as many different approaches to living a beautiful life as there are human beings in existence. For Schmid, to judge if one considers one's own life to be beautiful, one needs to take a 'step back' and reflect on one's life as a whole. One needs to ask the question if the life one has lived so far has overall led to a point where the person we have become is one that aligns with what we value – someone we can be proud of, or at least content with. Such a life, however, does not necessarily have to be one of ongoing happiness and constant mental, physical, emotional, social and spiritual wellbeing, as is often suggested to be important in the wellbeing discourse. In fact, the reader will be hard pressed to find any person alive that has not suffered from challenges, negative emotions, loss, or even despair. For Schmid, such experiences do not preclude one from judging one's life to be a beautiful one; on the opposite, one might reflect on how the hardships one has experienced have formed one's character and provided valuable insights into the complexity and beauty of life itself, and that these insights and the person one has become therefore made this a beautiful life overall. Hence, a life well lived can be a life that has seen significant periods without what is commonly described as 'wellbeing', as discussed above. To actively develop a beautiful life, according to Schmid, one needs to engage in and develop one's own *art of living*.

As indicated earlier, Schmid argues that to engage in an art of living means to take responsibility for one's own life, reflect on one's norms, values and beliefs, and endeavour to shape one's own life actively in accordance with these norms, values and beliefs one has deemed important for oneself. To engage in the art of living is further a life-long process; similar to the state of eudaimonia, one cannot stop at some point and find that one has achieved a beautiful life and there is nothing more to do. One would most likely just in that moment cease to have what one would consider a beautiful life to be. Stopping to actively shape one's own life would mean either to become driven by external forces or to die from not doing anything at all. In contrast to some of the terms and concepts discussed above, Schmid's notion of an art of living is therefore a life-long approach to being well. It also requires us to reflect on all our actions, habits and strivings in all aspects of our life in relation to what matters to us. Finally, it responds to Aristotle's notion of eudaimonia as it allows each of us to strive towards what we consider a beautiful life to be, which likely will allow us to reach a state of 'serene happiness' (Müller-Commichau, 2007) on occasion.

It needs to be said here, though, that Schmid's approach to an art of living does not necessarily follow a strict Aristotelian pathway of a virtuous life, as it allows a more flexible approach to personal held values and norms. This said, Schmid's ethics model (cf. Schmid, 2000; Teschers, 2018), based on Aristotle's notion of *phronésis* (prudence and practical wisdom)[9], suggests that individuals engaging in the art of living will come to understand the impact that extreme dispositions and actions, i.e., deficiencies on the one hand and excess on the other, can have on others and their ability to strive towards their own beautiful life. As such, these dispositions and actions can be in conflict with the *ethics of care* that individuals engaged in the art of living, according to Schmid, are likely to develop[10]. Therefore, Schmid seems to imply that to engage in the art of living will lead to a life that likely values moderation in many things, even though allowing for strongly held personal norms, values and beliefs to orient one's life. Schmid follows Aristotle, however, by arguing prudence and practical wisdom [German: Klugheit] to be a key faculty (or intellectual virtue) that allows the individual engaged in the art of living to navigate conflicting virtues, i.e., to make the right decision at the right time

---

9   For Aristotle, *phronesis* is a virtue of the mind, an example of the reasoning function of the 'soul'. In addition to mental or intellectual virtues, Aristotle proposes ethics or character virtues, which can be seen as dispositions of the 'soul' that are not part of reasoning per se but can still follow the reasoning of the mind (Kraut 2010).

10 Schmid's *ethics of care* or *ethics of practical wisdom* is based on an enlightened form of self-interest, through *phronésis*, that allows the individual to understand their relationship with and impact on the life of others, and that it is in their own best interest to care for others, society, humanity and our planet. This will be discussed further in Chapter 3.

and in the right way. I will expand this discussion further below and in relation to Biesta's (2022) approach to *world-centred education* in Chapter Five.

Considering each individual's journey towards an art of living, it needs to be acknowledged, though, that, according to Schmid (2000), engaging in an art of living does not require us to succeed in our endeavour to live a beautiful life. It just increases the likelihood of us considering our life to be beautiful, as at least we will have given it our 'best shot', so to say. It is hard to envision feeling a sense of eudaimonia if we look back at our life and feel a strong sense of regret because we have not tried actively to shape it into what we hoped it would be. Again, this does not mean that a beautiful life is a life without regrets, but it is a life that we can affirm in so far that we can be content with our effort if not with the outcome of every decision we have made. It is not, and will never be, a 'perfect life'.

An Art of Living Towards Personal and Community Wellbeing

As indicated above, to engage in an art of living means to live one's life actively and deliberately: it means to reflect on what is important to us and then to shape our actions and habits in line with what we value. Therefore, it is important for us to be able to critically reflect on messages we are given and values and norms that are circulated within the society and communities we are part of. A deliberate and conscious reflection on common values, norms and beliefs in the context of an art of living, however, also has a reciprocal effect back on our communities and society. Engaging in this way includes becoming *authentic* in one's actions towards oneself but also towards the people around us. It means to affirm values, norms and beliefs one consciously agrees with and to challenge those that conflict with what one stands for. In addition, Schmid (2000) explains that to engage in an art of living also means to be able to understand the interconnections of actions, reactions and consequences in the world, as well as to strive to reflect on causalities in our living environment. Causalities can be simple in some aspects that represent our physical world, but they are often quite hidden and difficult to work out in our social world. For example, questions of power and how actions of a person in one context affect people in another can be muddy and hard to follow. A recent example globally would be the Covid-19 pandemic and the responses of politicians, officials and each human being on the planet in relation to taking precautions, such as mask wearing, social distancing, and taking action to getting vaccinated to protect not just oneself but others in our communities as well. The impact of personal actions on a daily basis are hard to judge in terms of their impact locally, and even more so nationally and internationally. Further local examples would be the ongoing consequences of colonialisation – for example for Māori and Pākehā in the Aotearoa New Zealand context, Aborigines and Torrent Straight Islanders in Australia, first nations in North America, or the indigenous peoples of the Andes in Latin America[11] – the impact of historical events on people today, or the impact that current ideologies such as neoliberalism and the related concepts of marketization, performativity and accountability have on how people see themselves and their lives[12]. For Schmid, trying to reason through these complexities and understanding the impact of such matters on oneself will allow each person to act more purposefully and successfully to pursue their own version of a beautiful life and live in line with one's values, norms and beliefs.

To be able to work through these interconnections in the world one is living in depends, according to Schmid, on one's ability for prudence and practical wisdom – *phronésis*, as indicated above. Schmid explains that prudence and practical wisdom are required to understand many of the complexities of life and allows us to act purposefully in line with our values, norms and beliefs. However, it also helps us to shape and adjust our values and beliefs as we come to understand our living environment more fully. One part of this, as Schmid argues, is to understand that we are all part of a larger local, national and global community. Through prudence and practical wisdom, the self-interest of each individual will be transformed into, what Schmid calls, *enlightened self-interest*, which is to understand that our actions have consequences on others and will create reactions that again affect us and our ability to live a beautiful life. Therefore, Schmid reasons, engaging in an art of living means to come to understand that it is in our own best interest if we create a shared

---

11 I will draw on the Andean indigenous concept of *buen vivir* in relation to Schmid's art of living and education in Chapter 3.
12 See in this context Ching Lam's (2020) PhD research on *interbeing* in the context of Thích Nhất Hạnh's Engaged Buddhism. Interbeing here is the concept that everything and everyone is connected and inter-are, and as such affect each other. For example, the purchase of certain items and aspects of our lifestyle in Western countries has an effect on other people and places in our globalised world, including wars that are fought over resources and people that are working in slave-like conditions so that we can afford our next mobile phone and similar.

environment that supports each and every person to develop their own art of living and pursue their own beautiful life. Without being able to go into the complexity of this philosophical ethical theory here (see Chapters Three & Five for more details), Schmid explains how an enlightened care for oneself, as in developing one's own art of living, will result in a care for others around us, for our community, society and humanity as a whole. Through understanding the complex interplay of action and reaction, a person actively pursuing an art of living will come to understand how their actions today will impact on our environment and on other people here and now, as well as elsewhere and later on. Therefore, a person reflecting on one's values and desire to live a beautiful life will have to consider how their actions affect the ability of other people today, and our children in future, to pursue their own art of living. This notion also resonates with many indigenous worldviews, such as in te ao Māori and the notion of *buen vivir*, as I will discuss in the next chapter. As such, developing an art of living will mean not only a care for oneself and others, but also for our environment and our planet to allow current and future generations a stab at their own beautiful lives rather than a life of survival and hardship.

Therefore, what follows from the ability to understand the interconnectedness of things, events, actions and reactions in the world through *phronésis* – prudence and practical wisdom – can result in each person engaging in the art of living to strive for a more just, equal and fair society today, locally or globally, and to engage in more sustainable behaviour to protect our living environment and planet for us and future generations. As such, I would argue that taking a holistic art of living perspective, rather than a limited 'wellbeing' approach, will not only benefit individuals in their development here and now, but also have a larger impact on communities, societies and humanity today and in future. Even though it needs to be acknowledged that each individual's influence on a collective is limited. Therefore, a concerted effort and societal shift towards an art of living will likely be necessary.

Wellbeing, The Art of Living and Education

Having discussed the role and relationship between people's development of their own art of living and wellbeing for individuals, communities, societies, humanity and our planet, the question arises now *what* can be done *how* and *where* to support people in their pursuit of a beautiful life? One obvious answer would be the compulsory education system, as it arguably has the widest reach into society and can help people from a young age to gain the necessary skills, faculties and knowledge to develop their own art of living. I have argued before (Teschers, 2013, 2017, 2018) that an aim, if not an end of education, ought to be the development of people's own art of living to allow them to pursue the best possible, that is, the most beautiful life they can lead under the circumstances they are living in. To add to my earlier philosophical arguments why a beautiful life ought to be an end of education, a practical point can be made here in relation to the topic of 'wellbeing'. As *being well* or *living well* in Aristotle's *eudemonic* sense seems to be a key driver for human beings, and as the engagement with the art of living and pursuit of one's own beautiful life arguably can lead to personal 'wellbeing' in a wider sense – as well as to increased levels of social and community wellbeing, justice and fairness – shifting the focus of education systems towards supporting the development of an art of living seems prudent.

Considering that neoliberal ideology (among others, expressed through marketisation and consumerism approaches to education) is still strongly reflected in Aotearoa New Zealand's and many other countries' dominant cultural environment, I argue that focusing compulsory education on the development of each student's art of living should appeal to advocates of both sides of the divide between education being a private versus a public good. While there is strong evidence and arguments in support of higher levels of education benefiting a society as a whole (Locatelli, 2019), the neoliberal ideology positioning education as a private good to be consumed (and paid for) by individuals for their own gain is still prevailing in the public and political discourse in many countries. However, either position should consider an art of living approach to education desirable due to the potential to improve the lives of individuals and consequently the social cohesion of a society through raising the wellbeing of both individuals and society, as indicated above and argued further in Chapter Three.

Having proposed reasons for the *why*, now I would like to make some brief remarks on the *how* of shifting the focus in education towards the development of students' own art of living, points I will expand on further in later chapters. I want to place the emphasis on the term *shift* rather than 'change', as it would not necessarily require a complete overhaul of the education system and curriculum. Shifting the focus will result in some structural changes in how curriculum, pedagogy and assessment are conceptualised; it does not mean to completely change the system but, rather, to rethink our approach to education and the education system from an art of living perspective. This includes reviewing national education policies, strategies and guidelines with an eye on how we can create an educational environment that is conducive to the development of students' own art of living. Unquestionably, the ability to navigate today's world and society, as well as the ability to take up a meaningful job are significant aspects of students' ability to strive towards a beautiful life; however, by no means should the ability to take up a job that contributes to the national GDP be seen anymore as the sole or even main focus of education, as argued, for example, by Biesta (2022). Other neoliberally inspired instruments, such as 'National Standards' (already abolished by the Labour Government in Aotearoa in 2017, which might indicated a slow shift away from neoliberal mindsets) and 'league tables' of school performance linked to national indicators will likely lose importance with a shift of thinking focused on the wellbeing and holistic development of our next generations.

Such a shift in thinking would further support other movements within the social and educational landscape, such as efforts focused on inclusive education (understood here as a holistic approach rather than merely focused on learning disability) and more equity within education (see Chapters Four & Six for more details). I would argue that foregrounding the wellbeing and personal development of students' own beautiful life, based on their backgrounds, interests and aspirations, will likely contribute to students seeing the relevance of schooling for their own lives. This can further support the development of a sense of self and belonging to a school community, which are also linked to increased engagement and learning in schools, especially for marginalised groups (Singh et al., 2008; Rahman, 2013). This could potentially counter the negative impact of neoliberal structures such as marketization, performativity and accountability on students' mental health and sense of self (Nairn, Sligo & Higgins, 2012; Fleming et al., 2020), and ultimately strengthen their wellbeing in both the common narrow and the wider holistic understanding, as proposed here.

Following the why and the how, I will now outline briefly a few implications – the *what* – for curriculum and classroom practice, which I will expand further in Chapter Six. These suggestions made here will be rather broad, as curriculum and pedagogy need to be adjusted for each classroom and student context; however, these contemplations might give the interested reader an idea where to start and what could be done today without waiting for top-down changes of educational policy and national curricula. The two key areas that apply to classroom practice, and can be redesigned by teachers and schools, are *curriculum* and *pedagogy*. While it is possible for this to be done by individual teachers and classroom settings, I have argued earlier that such an approach would be much more impactful if it was handled on a whole school basis to create a school-wide environment that supports the development of peoples' own art of living (Teschers, 2018: 152).

Regarding the curriculum, Schmid (2000) proposes a number of larger topic areas that are relevant for students in today's modern (and post-modern) societies to allow students to engage critically with the globalised, diverse and interconnected reality many people are living in:

> the human being as individual; the social human being; difficulties and burdens of human life; striving for fulfilment and meaning in life; religions, beliefs and cultures of humanity; and the personal shape of life and global perspectives. (Teschers, 2018: 120, italics removed)

While this list is likely not exhaustive, as will be discussed further in later chapters, it provides a starting point to review current curriculum content from a human development focused perspective to fill gaps of knowledge and understanding relevant for an art of living that might not be covered in existing curricula yet. Other aspects that are of importance for the development of students' own art of living are the abilities of critical thinking and self-reflection; imagination and creativity; prudence and practical wisdom and, overall, the ability to look critically at the interconnections in the world and the impact history, current settings and circumstances, actions, dispositions and power relations have on people and events in the world. To develop these abilities, a certain understanding of the world is needed, which is partly reflected in the curriculum topics identified above, and can partly be addressed through pedagogy, as I will discuss in Chapter Six.

Conclusion

In this chapter, I have critiqued the often limited scope of the term 'wellbeing' as it is used in relation to educational policy and practice. A narrow understanding of wellbeing based on medical and health models in regard to mental and physical wellbeing, possibly incorporating emotional wellbeing, tend to fall short to consider the *life-wide* complexities of human being striving for *eudaimonia* in their lives. And a time-constrained understanding of wellbeing in the moment, or even considering the recent past again tends to emphasise a (mental) health understanding of wellbeing in the hedonic sense of 'feeling well' and experiencing more positive emotions than negative ones – in general or in relation to education and schooling. A *life-long* approach to wellbeing in education, encompassing the past but also the future of our students by considering their aspirations, norms and values, can support students to develop more fully as human beings who pursue their vision of a beautiful life that might lead to *eudaimonia*. Further, placing a holistic approach to the wellbeing of students that includes life-wide and life-long perspectives at the centre, such as in an art of living approach to education, can contribute not only to our students' but also our society's wellbeing, equity and fairness. Considering equal educational opportunity and equity through an art of living perspective will further shift the judging criteria of what is 'fair' and 'just' from external measurements to the internal perspective of each student, which I will expand on in Chapter Four. I also suggested that supporting the development of people's art of living can support societal values of tolerance, support, fairness and justice, which can lead to increased wellbeing for individuals, communities and societies. The authenticity of our habits, our *gestures* as Schmid calls them, in relation to our norms, values and beliefs is a signature trait of actively shaping one's own life as understood in Schmid's art of living approach, which ultimately will increase the likelihood for us to reach *eudaimonia* – a state of serene happiness and holistic wellbeing. In the following chapter, I will expand on the relationship of the art of living for individual and societal good, drawing on Western philosophy and indigenous traditions.

Acknowledgement

This chapter, with permission, incorporates material from a previous book chapter 'Education towards a beautiful life in an imperfect world'. In Kamp et al. (Eds.), (2023) *Wellbeing – Global Policies and Perspectives. Insights from Aotearoa New Zealand and beyond.* Peter Lang.

References

Aristotle. (1996). *The Nicomachean ethics.* Edited by T. Griffith. London, England: Wordsworth Editions Limited.
Biesta, G. (2013). *The beautiful risk of education.* Paradigm.
Biesta, G. (2022). *World-centred education: A view for the present.* Routledge.
Busseri, M. A., & Sadava, S. W. (2011). A review of the tripartite structure of subjective wellbeing: Implications for conceptualization, operationalization, analysis, and synthesis. *Personality and Social Psychology Review, 15*(3), 290–314. doi:10.1177/1088868310391271.

Fleming, T. et al. (2020). *Youth19 Rangatahi Smart Survey, Initial Findings: Hauora Hinengaro / Emotional and Mental Health*, The Youth19 Research Group, The University of Auckland and Victoria University of Wellington.

Kamp, A., Brown, C., O'Toole, V., & McMenamin, T. (Eds.) (2023). Wellbeing: Global Policies and Perspectives. Peter Lang.

Kraut, R. (2010). Aristotle's ethics. In E.N. Zalta (Ed.), *The Stanford encyclopedia of philosophy*. Available at: http://plato.stanford.edu/archives/sum2010/entries/aristotle-ethics/.

Kristjánsson, K. (2012). 'Positive psychology and positive education: Old wine in new bottles?'. *Educational Psychologist, 47*(2), 86–105. doi:10.1080/00461520.2011.610678.

Kristjánsson, K. (2019). *Flourishing as the aim of education, flourishing as the aim of education*. New York, NY: Routledge. doi:10.4324/9780429464898.

Lam, Y. C. (2020). *Mindfulness, Interbeing and the Engaged Buddhism of Thích Nhất Hạnh*. PhD Thesis. University of Canterbury, New Zealand. doi:10.26021/11115.

Locatelli, R. (2019). *Reframing education as a public and common good*. Cham: Springer International Publishing. doi:10.1007/978-3-030-24801-7.

Müller-Commichau, W. (2007). *Lebenskunst lernen*. Baltmannsweiler, Germany: Schneider.

Nairn, K. M., Sligo, J., & Higgins, J. (2012). *Children of Rogernomics : A neoliberal generation leaves school*. Dunedin, N.Z.: Otago University Press.

Noddings, N. (2013). *Caring: A relational approach to ethics & moral education* (2nd ed.). University of California Press.

Rahman, K. (2013) 'Belonging and learning to belong in school: the implications of the hidden curriculum for indigenous students', *Discourse, 34*(5), 660–672. doi:10.1080/01596306.2013.728362.

Roberts, P. (2016). *Happiness, hope, and despair: Rethinking the role of education*. Peter Lang.

Sandholm, D. et al. (2022). Teachers' experiences with positive education. *Cambridge Journal of Education*, 1–19. doi:10.1080/0305764X.2022.2093839.

Schmid, W. (2000). *Philosophie der Lebenskunst: Eine Grundlegung*. Frankfurt: Suhrkamp.

Seligman, M. E. P. (2010). *Authentic happiness: Using the new positive psychology to realise your potential for lasting fulfillment*. London, England: Nicholas Brealey Publishing.

Seligman, M. E. P. (2011). *Flourish: A visionary new understanding of happiness and well-being*. New York, NY: Free Press.

Singh, K., Mido, C., & Dika, S. (2008). School engagement and school learning: Ethnicity, self-concept, and school belonging. *International Journal of Learning, 15*(2), 205–213. Available at: https://proxy.library.csi.cuny.edu/login?url=http://search.ebscohost.com/login.aspx?direct=true&db=ehh&AN=34382003&site=ehost-live.

Suissa, J. (2008). Lessons from a new science? On teaching happiness in schools. *Journal of Philosophy of Education, 42*(3–4), 575–590. Available at: http://www.cambridgewellbeing.

Sun, R. C. F., & Shek, D. T. L. (2014). Well-being, student. *Encyclopedia of Quality of Life and Well-Being Research*, 7103–7108. doi:10.1007/978-94-007-0753-5_2891.

Teschers. (2013). An educational approach to the art of living. *Knowledge Cultures, 1*(2), 25–32.

Teschers, C. (2017). A BEAUTIFUL LIFE AS AN END OF EDUCATION. *Knowledge Cultures, 5*(6), 62–73. doi:10.22381/KC5620175.

Teschers, C. (2018). *Education and Schmid's art of living, education and Schmid's art of living*. Routledge. doi:10.4324/9781315563848.

Vidal, W. E., & O'Steen, B. (2023). What counts as wellbeing? In A. Kamp et al. (Eds.), *Wellbeing. Global policies and perspectives* (pp. 11–34). Peter Lang.

White, M., & Murray, S. (2015). *Evidence-based approaches in positive education: Implementing a strategic framework for well-being in schools*. Edited by M. White and S. Murray. Springer.

· 3 ·

THE ART OF LIVING FOR INDIVIDUAL AND COMMUNITY GOOD

As indicated in Chapter Two, an education for an art of living can have positive implications not only for the wellbeing of the individual but also for the good of a community, society, and the environment. In this chapter, I will expand on this idea by discussing Schmid's ethics for an art of living in more detail and outlining a vision for possible implications if the art of living was embraced in earnest by most members of a community or society. I will further draw links between Schmid's art of living and related concepts from other cultural contexts, most notably the indigenous concept of *buen vivir* from the Andean peoples in the Americas, as well as the notion of *Mauri Ora* and *tikanga* in te ao Māori – aspects of wellbeing and guidelines of how to act in life in the worldview of the Māori people in Aotearoa New Zealand.

Schmid's Ethics for an Art of Living and Notions of 'Good'

The question of how one should live, or ought to live, has been pondered throughout history[1]. Going back to the earliest preserved writings in Western philosophy, Socrates claimed that to live a good life means, one should strive for a life of a philosopher: pursue and love wisdom and

---

1 I am listing a few examples here to illustrate the point, while not having the scope to discuss any of these in any meaningful way. I hope the knowledgeable reader will excuse my brevity.

truth. Aristotle (1996), arguably the most influential philosopher to date in relation to ethics and moral values, proposed a virtues ethics, suggesting that a 'good life' is a life of virtues: following the moderate path, not sliding into extremes at either side of dispositions or actions, but to maintain a balanced approach, guided by rational thinking (Kraut, 2010). While Aristotle focuses on the human ability of rational thinking[2] as distinctly human and, therefore, a key aspect of what it means to live a 'good life' and to reach a state of *eudaimonia* (utmost happiness), Epicurus, for example, focused more on our emotional experiences, in what philosophers often call a *hedonic* life, a life of pleasures (Feldman, 2004). While much has been written in either tradition, accounts of living a good life seem generally to fall somewhere on the spectrum between Aristotle's *eudemonic* and Epicurus' *hedonic* approach (e.g., Seligman, 2011; Kristjánsson, 2012; Vidal & O'Steen, 2023).

A different way of looking at the question of a 'good life' would be the criteria that we apply for 'good'. Feldman (2004: 8–9), for example, lists a number of aspects such as (i) morally and/or ethically good; (ii) good in terms of biological function of human beings in the context of evolution – what it means to be human in contrast to other animals (arguably Aristotle's starting position); (iii) aesthetically good, as in a biography that seems well rounded and 'beautiful' from an outside perspective; (iv) emotionally and experientially good – what Feldman links to 'wellbeing' (e.g., Epicurus' hedonic tradition); or (v) 'causally good', a life that is *beneficial* to others (Feldman refers to Mother Theresa as example here). I would like to add the financially good life, i.e., a life of wealth and amenities, to this list as it seems reflective of the Zeitgeist in our current neoliberally driven, consumeristic societal context, perpetuated through the advertisement industry, trying to instil the believe that possessions and consumerism can lead to 'happiness' and a 'good life'[3]. I would also like to draw attention to point (v) in the list above, as the social and community care understanding seems closer aligned with indigenous views on living a good life, which I will discuss in more detail later on in this chapter.

---

2 Although it needs to be acknowledged that Aristotle does not see emotions as opposed to reason but partly as constitutive of it; as such, I do not want to claim a clear dichotomy here but alert to a level of emphasis.

3 However, Aristotle (1996) dismisses this idea quickly as he argues money to only have instrumental value.

Considering the existing connotations and possible ways of understanding the term 'good life', Wilhelm Schmid (2000b) deliberately opted for the term *beautiful life* instead of 'good'. As mentioned earlier in this book, Schmid argues that what it means to live a beautiful life lies in the eyes of the beholder. Like a piece of art, whether a life is considered beautiful remains a question of personal taste rather than set external criteria or expectations. As such, Schmid captures and validates the myriad of different pathways and experiences in life without necessarily creating a prescriptive hierarchy of which life might be 'better' or 'more beautiful' than another. This approach of his art of living concept of placing the individual living their life as the judge of their own life allows each person to take a step back and reflect on the life they have lived to date and decide if they would consider it to be a beautiful life or not, based on their personally held norms, values, and beliefs. In contrast to some of the conceptions of a 'good life', as outlined above, this approach is less exclusive and judgemental from the outside and allows for divergent norms, values, and beliefs – different experiences in life to be considered as beautiful by the person living said life.

As one example, a person who experienced significant hardship in their life, maybe lost people significant to them or experienced a challenging illness or a form of disability that severely limits their ability and choices in life, might still be able to look back at their life and say: 'it may not have been a happy or easy life, but I am content with where my path has taken me, the choices I have made in line with my values and beliefs, and I can embrace the person I have become due to the experiences I have had'. From the outside, such a life would possibly not be seen as 'good' in terms of happiness, wellbeing, emotional pleasures, or possibly financial achievements, to name only some. However, despite (or maybe because of) the circumstances, the person might still feel that their life overall has been beautiful in relation to their norms, values, beliefs, and aspirations they hold and the experiences they made and cherished that might not be apparent from the outside. Relating to this is Peter Roberts (2016) work about the role of despair for education and human development. Negative emotions, sorrow, despair, and challenging life experiences can be quite educational and be much more influential in shaping a person – their character – than a life of ongoing happiness and pleasures might. Challenges in life invite us, or even demand from us, to adapt and develop – to push our boundaries and *become* as a human being: to shape ourselves and our lives actively. As such, these experiences can be instrumental, if not foundational, for a person's *subjectification*, to use Biesta's (2013) term here – to become an active self with agency rather than a clone of societal expectations and beliefs. Agency, however, also sits at the heart of Schmid's art of living, which is to take responsibility for one's own life (not be driven by external expectations and forces alone) and attempting to actively shape their life into what they would consider a beautiful life to be. In contrast, a supposedly 'good life' consisting of a string of pleasures, positive experiences, and constant consumption of 'new things', as might be suggested by some societal and cultural norms and beliefs of our time, might lead to a passive life, driven by external expectations, which, on reflection, might be considered as hollow or empty when looked at it seriously and by taking a step back by the person living said life. This is not to say that this person might not judge their life to be beautiful, but only when their personal norms, values and beliefs fully align with the external expectations that have driven their life to that point. To make this judgement then, however, would require the individual to actively reflect on their norms, values, and beliefs in this instant, which arguably could be seen as a transition point from being driven by external forces to taking agency and responsibility for one's own life in this moment. What comes next would then determine if this person becomes an active 'artist' shaping their own life or reverts back into being driven by external expectations and social norms. In this context, Peter Bieri (2006) considers a person being driven by external expectations and not taking charge of their own life an experience of un-freedom, whereas taking charge of one's own life, under the circumstances and restrictions one might be living in, would rather constitute a life towards freedom. As such, engagement with the art of living can also be considered an act of emancipation and towards a form of personal, internal freedom notwithstanding the external constrains one might find oneself living in.

However, an ethical issue arises from these considerations and Schmid's individualistic approach to an art of living: the question what happens if someone's concept of a 'beautiful life' unduly encroaches on the life of other people. An example that has been brought up again and again by colleagues is the axe-murder example: what if someone sees their beautiful life to be an axe-murderer? While somewhat extreme, other examples can come to mind, such as what about stealing, or taking advantage of others in a myriad of ways? – Here, one wonders though which, if any of these examples, would actually fall under an art of living approach and Schmid's concept of a 'beautiful life' in the first place. And even if it would, this does not mean that a society needs to accept and enable such approaches to life as it would not be in the best interest of the collective (community, society, or humanity) to do so and limit other members' ability to live a good life. As such, the social contract and rules of a society negotiating peaceful co-existence do not have to be abandoned by society. Competing interests between individual members of any community will always have to be negotiated. However, some of these rules might adjust slightly when approached from an art of living perspective, which could be seen as a subsection of a social layer of practical ethics as discussed in earlier work (cf. Teschers, 2018: 71–72).

Schmid's (2000b) answer to this question lies in Aristotle's aforementioned notion of *phronésis* – prudence and practical wisdom. As explained in the earlier chapters, a critical faculty of Schmid's art of living concept is the ability for *phronésis*. According to Schmid, prudence and practical wisdom will allow the individual engaged in the art of living to identify and understand (many of) the interconnections in the world, which again allows them to actively effect change, i.e., shape their own life and take meaningful action in line with their norms, values, and beliefs. As part of this understanding of the interconnections, the individual engaged in the art of living will understand that actions that impact on other members of society unduly are likely to be sanctioned by society (e.g., punishment in form of loss of resources or freedom to act), which will likely reduce their ability to pursue their version of a beautiful life in the first place. Further, Schmid argues, through *phronésis* one will come to understand that the likelihood of living a life close to what one would consider a beautiful life to be is increased if one lives in an environment that is conducive to the development of an art of living, and potentially a beautiful life, for all. Therefore, it is in the own best interest of each individual to act in a way that supports others around them in the pursuit of their own art of living and beautiful life. Schmid calls this the transformation from an egoistic form of self-interest to a form of *enlightened self-interest*, which realises that the interests of others around us and society in general are relevant to our own interests and therefore *their consideration is part* of our own self-interest. Schmid, therefore, develops here an individual ethics approach, which he proposes could be called *ethics of practical wisdom* [German: Ethik der Klugheit/Klugheitsethik].

Expanding on this reasoning, Schmid states that what starts with a care for the self (Schmid drawing on Foucault 1984) will, through prudence and practical wisdom, develop into a care for others, a care for society, a care for humanity and a care for the planet and our environment, as the individual engaged in the art of living will realise all these relate to and are relevant for their own self-interest to pursue a beautiful life. Schmid concedes, however, that due to the lessened impact of expanding circles on one's own life, one would have to value the continued existence of humanity itself to arrive at the broadest circles of care. For example, while one might still care for one's immediate environment that significantly affects one's life in the here and now, a care for the planet as a whole is likely too removed to have any significant impact on one's own life but becomes more relevant again if one values a good living environment for following generations of human beings (such values can be held regardless of one having children oneself or not). This said, considering the likely impacts of global warming and other environmental crises across the globe, the effects of human action on people's life here and now seem much more tangible today than they have been in the past. As such, a care for the planet might be easier to develop now than in previous generations as the effects of our actions in the past have become much more salient, understandable and immediate for many. It is also necessary to alert to cultural differences here, as, for example, various Indigenous peoples of Latin America as well as Māori in Aotearoa New Zealand in their cultural tradition see the care for 'mother earth', our planet and environment, as paramount and arguably have a stronger connection to place and environment than people brought up in 'Western' cultural contexts.

However, despite the circles of care that the enlightened individual will realise, practical observation of people's actions on a daily basis – and many examples throughout history – seem to indicate that even people who can be seen as reasonably logical and able of rational and critical thought often act in ways that are in conflict with the expanding circles of care for others, society or the environment. Some possible explanations come to mind: Firstly, people acting in such ways may not have reached a level of prudence and practical wisdom, i.e., an understanding of what is the right thing to do at the right time and the right context, to move from egoistic self-interest – from an 'infantile' ego-logical state of being (Biesta, 2022) – to a form of *enlightened self-interest* (Schmid, 2000b), or what Biesta would call: a 'grown up' eco-logical, world-centred, approach to being. Or, secondly, they might not have applied their rationality and critical thinking skills in a reflective way on the values, norms, and beliefs they hold and/or how their actions align with their self-reflected values. Either situation would call for support in developing their art of living through the development of *phronésis* and the habit of self-reflection of their norms, values, beliefs, and actions (or 'gestures' as Schmid call them; German: Gestik). A third reason could be, however, that the societal and cultural circumstances one finds oneself in are hindering to fully align one's actions with one's norms, values, and beliefs. An example would be that travel by car is a necessity for many and alternative modes of transportation might not always be available or feasible. Costs for electric cars, however, are at the time of writing this book still somewhat prohibitive for many. And there are the other ethical complexities of worker exploitation for rare metals, for example, to consider which might compete with one's desire to act sustainable in life. Hence, one needs to concede that authentic action might be limited to relative action, not absolute, in relation to one's norms, values, and beliefs until such time where societal (and technical) structures allow for increasing levels of appropriate and authentic action. This said, there is probably much most of us could do today to strive towards living more in line with our held norms, values, and beliefs, even though it might create a level of discomfort at times.

Links Between Schmid's Art of Living and Indigenous Worldviews[4]

In previous research with colleagues (Teschers & Nieto, 2023), we have explored links between Schmid's concept of the art of living, based on predominantly traditional Western philosophy, and selected indigenous worldviews and approaches to living a 'good' or 'beautiful' life. An interesting connecting point that emerged, particularly in relation to individual and community 'good', has been Schmid's *ethics of practical wisdom*. While not the only connection – and it needs to be pointed out that significant differences exist between Schmid's philosophy and indigenous worldviews – Schmid's ethics model of expanding circles of care connects well with the layers of care

---

4 I want to acknowledge here that my account of *buen vivir* is based on the shared work by Dr Nieto and myself (Teschers and Nieto 2023) and largely informed by Dr Nieto's work and interpretation of the concept based on her understanding of the body of literature written in Spanish, as well as her conversations with selected indigenous participants in Columbia as part of a larger study we are conducting on cultural understandings of an art of living in various countries and cultures.

and consideration in regard to human action in, for example, the concept of *buen vivir* [good living], which is based on the traditions of the indigenous peoples of Latin America, as well as with shared values and worldviews of the indigenous Māori in Aotearoa New Zealand. I will start with a summary of our findings of comparing the art of living with *buen vivir* before commenting on links to Māori worldviews.

While the term '*buen vivir*' has been coined only recently towards the end of the 20th century, it is strongly influenced by long historical traditions of the indigenous peoples in the Americas, such as the Kichwa, the Aymara, the Maya, the Guarani and the Nasa peoples. Cultural concepts resembling the core of the current notion of *buen vivir* can be found in the traditions of each of these peoples, even though they are not all the same and differences in the detail of what sits behind these cultural concepts exist. As such, *buen vivir* is a contemporary interpretation of longstanding ancestral cultural traditions, put in dialogue with each other as well as in dialogue with current Western concepts and values. It has therefore seen popularity beyond indigenous populations including mezino (non-indigenous) people and political leaders. However, it needs to be noted that the current interpretation can lack the depth and complexities of concepts represented in the historical indigenous traditions (cf. Prage, 2015). Notwithstanding the differences in traditional indigenous cultural concepts, *buen vivir* is generally regarded to encompass values, principles and practices that support living a 'good' and possibly a 'beautiful life'. Hence the interest in exploring connections and differences between this concept and Schmid's art of living. In the following, I will provide a short overview of some of the values and principles of *buen vivir* and how they link with Schmid's art of living, with a particular view on how individual good and community good interrelate in both. To do this, I will draw on two indigenous concepts on which *buen vivir* is based: *Sumak Kawsay* (Kichwa people, Ecuador/Perú) and *Lekil Kuxlejal* (Maya people, Mexico).

According to Kowii (2015), Sumak Kawsay reflects the ancestral understanding of a good and beautiful life, where Sumak means 'the ideal, the beautiful and the good, the realisation' and Kawsay means 'life' concerning a 'life that is dignified, in harmony and equilibrium with the universe and the human beings' (p. 5)[5]. Likewise, Tortosa (2009) explains that Sumak Kawsay expresses the idea of a 'life not [in itself] better, nor better than that of others, nor a continuous urge to improve it, but simply good in all its aspects' (p. 1).

---

5   Please note that all translations from Spanish into English from sources quoted in this section have been provided by my colleague Dr Maria Nieto.

Tortosa stirs away from neoliberal considerations of comparison and (self-) maximisation and emphasises 'goodness' as both ethically good and good in terms of diligence and doing things well. Hence, both Kowii and Tortosa suggest that Sumak Kawsay is an ancestral worldview about how a good life should be lived, which does not require aspects of (self-)maximisation or constant improvement (possessions), and it is not measured in comparison to other people but measured against other criteria. While some of these aspects resonate well with Schmid's take of a beautiful life, the criteria of what constitutes 'good' in the indigenous context needs further exploration. Schmid emphasises the individual, personal perspective as measure of a beautiful life rather than any external criteria. I will comment further on this below.

According to Kowii (2015) and Tortosa (2009), a good life is beautiful and harmonious, while living a good life entails coherency between attitudes and practices – a notion that is mirrored in Schmid's understanding of an art of living where actions should align with personal norms, values and beliefs. Moreover, the principles and values of Sumak Kawsay are properly understood when they are enacted in life responsive to each situation and context: 'El Buen Vivir se logra haciendo bien las cosas' [Good Living is achieved, when one is doing things well] (Durán López, 2010: 59). Durán's interpretation of 'well' in this context seems to mean 'doing what is appropriate', including both being aware of the context to act ethically right, i.e., *doing the right thing*, and being aware and focused on what one is doing to act in a diligent way, i.e., *doing things right*. As such, there is some connection to Aristotle's notion of *phronésis* as it is used by Schmid, as the first aspect could be related to practical wisdom, the second to prudence[6].

Prage (2015) connects the principles of Sumak Kawsay with the principles, values and practices of *Lekil kuxlejal*, which is an expression in Tsotsil and Tseltal, two of the Mayan languages spoken in Chiapas (Mexico). She maintains that 'Lekil translates as good, kuxlejal as life' (p. 5). According to Prage, Lekil kuxlejal is usually translated as 'Good Living, living well or a dignified life' and involves many aspects, such as autonomy, the recognition of all living beings, harmony between humans as well as between humans and nature (p. 5).

---

6 Prudence and Practical Wisdom are both terms that are related but somewhat different in meaning and used to translate *phronésis* in English – prudence as the ability to know what to do to achieve a goal, practical wisdom to know what the ethically right thing is to do in any situation. Arguably, the German term 'Klugheit', used by Schmid as translation for phronésis, also includes these two meanings.

In relation to Schmid's ethics of practical wisdom, Prage (2015) discusses three dimensions of Lekil kuxlejal: first is 'the centrality of earth' or the 'recognition of earths' subjectivity' (p. 20); second is social justice; and third is government. Within the first dimension, three associated values are reciprocity, happiness and spirituality. Within the second dimension, the central value is dignity, or to acknowledge the greatness in all beings, not only humans but every living thing. Such dignity, in turn, requires respect and the awakening of a conscience within the Indigenous communities that they have rights to claim, thus, 'making people questioning their own situation' (p. 36). Within the third dimension, the central value is autonomy expressed in the struggle for autonomous health and education within their cosmovision. These three dimensions that move from the outside in, from the macrocosm to the microcosm so to say, is mirrored in reverse in Schmid's ethics model of the art of living. In Schmid's model, he builds, as discussed above, on the enlightened self-interest of the individual who, through *phronésis*, comes to understand that they need to care for the people and community surrounding them and the environment we are living in. While the starting position of these two approaches are reversed, arguably there is common ground in the shared dimensions they both come to value[7], as will be discussed in more detail below.

Similarities and Differences in the Tradition of Values, Norms and Beliefs

The values, principles and practices of each Indigenous culture that relate to the notion of *buen vivir* derive from ancient cultural knowledge. Mainly oral traditions allow for intergenerational transmission of such knowledge. Each Indigenous culture introduces the new generations to living a good life by engaging with adults in the daily activities where actions are to be performed according to the respective values and principles (Prage, 2015: 6).

This relates to Schmid's concept insofar as the art of living includes an alignment between one's norms, values and beliefs with the actions one takes, one's gestures and habitus (Schmid, 2000a). However, Schmid points out that to develop one's own art of living and actively shaping one's own life, one has to reflect on the norms, values, beliefs and principles society is offering us. As such, while learning the values and principles that are seen by a people

---

7 It needs to be acknowledged here that the Indigenous model indicates a much deeper interpretation and relationship with the world, people and oneself than Schmid's ethics model suggests.

or a group as contributing to a 'good life', a person engaged in the art of living will reflect on these values and principles and actively decide if these traditions conform to one's personal views on life and the personal values one holds. If they do align, one can actively accept them into shaping one's life in such a manner, but if certain values and principles of the past do not resonate with one's personal view of life and how one wants to live one's life, active engagement in the art of living will mean to adjust or abandon these. This said, Schmid also points out that an individual engaged in the art of living will periodically reflect on their own norms, values and beliefs, which can change through the experiences we make and the subsequent personal development as a human being. As such, traditional values, principles and the handed down wisdom of a people might influence one's worldview and what it means to live a good and beautiful life, but they need to be actively tested by each person before being accepted and incorporated into their own life. So, while there are connecting points in so far as people in any cultural setting are exposed to cultural norms and values, Schmid emphasises the need to reflect on them and make decisions on a personal basis rather than a communal basis. In Indigenous communities, such adjustments to cultural values to changing times will more likely be negotiated in a communal sense and a slow adaptation of traditional values to a changing environment (cf. Viasus, Posada & Díaz, 2016).

Valuing and Enacting a Care for Others and Community

According to the authors reviewed above in this context, the principles and values of good living are still part of life today of indigenous communities. However, the authors agree that the connections with ancestral knowledge is fragile and in danger of being lost. Specifically, the relationship between human and nature is a fundamental part of buen vivir, and that relation 'has now been degraded' (Prage, 2015: 21) in the more contemporary understanding of the term and the changed environment in Latin America through colonialisation.

This resembles a clash of worldviews between traditional communal approaches to good living and the dominating neoliberal ideology promoting individualism and self-maximisation as a mantra for living a 'good life', which is strongly present in many countries in the Americas as well as most of the Western world. The notion of *buen vivir* has been suggested as a counter to these neoliberal agendas (Esteva, 2011; Houtart, 2011; Prage, 2015; Rico,

2019), which links with Schmid's concept of an art of living that requires each individual, through prudence and practical wisdom to develop a care for others, society, humanity and the planet. As such, Schmid's art of living approach can be positioned as one way that, while starting with the self-interest of the individual, transforms each person engaged in the process to take a more holistic and caring approach, acknowledging that to be able to live a beautiful life is strongly connected to the ability of other people and the wider community and society to also be able to shape their own versions of a beautiful life. As such, a care for others and the community surrounding oneself is an important aspect of Schmid's art of living in a similar way as it is a requirement for Indigenous people to uphold the depth of their own culture and shared understanding of how to practice *buen vivir*.

'Goodness' in Buen Vivir and the 'Beautiful Life'

Quijano (2012) argues that the 'goodness' of life in the cosmovision of the Indigenous peoples of Latin America differs substantially from the ideas of a 'good life' as meaning comfort and increased access to material goods, which is typical in a capitalist/Western socio-economic approach. Quijano (2012), echoing Medina (2006), argues that the 'goodness' inherent in Sumak Kawsay, for example, refers to a life characterised by balance, sufficiency, beauty and inclusion (of people, gods and nature). This alternative take on what a 'good life' might be, resonates with Schmid's critique of the pre-conception of the term in the public consciousness in Western (and other) societies, as outlined above. Schmid has argued that such, often narrow, preconceptions of a good life as comfortable, pleasurable, and 'happy' through consumption do not reflect the wide variety of life concepts. Similarly, positive psychology research has shown that these preconceptions of monetary wealth and the pursuit of a narrow form of pleasures as so-called 'happiness' can be misleading and do not necessarily include what gives people meaning in life or increases their life-satisfaction overall (Boniwell, 2008). Schmid, therefore, uses the term 'beautiful life' to indicate that views on what makes a life 'good' or worthwhile living are subjective as it is a work of art. While this subjective notion of a beautiful life is not synonymous with the notion of goodness as described by Quijano and Medina, both approaches offer a critique of common popular conceptions of a good life having to include accumulation of wealth and the pursuit of amenities, pleasures, and happiness. In fact, the call for austerity and affection in Sumak Kawsay (Quijano, 2012) for others links with early

Epicurean forms of hedonism, which did not proclaim the pursuit of excessive pleasures but rather to take enjoyment from the simple pleasures in life, such as the enjoyment of a sustaining simple meal or the company of a good friend (Feldman, 2004). Returning to Schmid's work, I want to re-emphasise that the Aristotelian notion of *phronésis*, which Schmid sees as central to an art of living, has been argued to lead each person developing an art of living to consider the impact of their actions on others and the environment. This will, therefore, lead to considerations of balance and prudent use of resources in the best interest of all, which links again to the notion of inclusion as indicated by Medina above. Therefore, Schmid's art of living, despite its starting point at the self-interest of the individual, has the promise to develop a similar view towards the good of the community and environment as the indigenous notion of *buen vivir* has.

The Relationship Between Community, Individual and Environment

Burgos (2016) notes that *buen vivir* is an understanding of life where the community aspect prevails: 'It does not admit a good life of a few people accumulating wealth at the expense of many who fail' (p. 189). Similarly, Prage (2015) notes that the concepts of Lekil Kuxlejal [good life/dignified life] and Sumak Kawsay [*buen vivir*; good living] are to some extent 'equivalent' as both emphasise the collective (p. 8). Here, again, we can find links to Schmid's ethics model and the necessity to consider others and the care for others through *phronésis*. Being part of a community and society requires the individual to consider the good of the community to create an environment that is conducive to the development of their own art of living and beautiful life, which will make it also conducive to the development and pursuit of other people's beautiful lives. So, while Schmid in the art of living does not emphasise the primacy of the collective as an inherent value, through the insight of prudence and practical wisdom the individual engaged in the art of living will understand that undue accumulation of wealth and resources at the expense of others can effectively hinder the pursuit of their own beautiful life, which consequently (and I maybe naively optimistic here) could lead to more equity and social justice within a community and/or society.

Authors such as Houtart (2011), Kowii (2015) and Medina (2001) emphasise that across the Indigenous people of Latin America the notion of *interdependence* is a central value in *buen vivir*. This means the recognition of the inherent worth of every creature and how our life depends on the well-being of others. This principle also implies an understanding of how different forms of life depend on one another. Moreover, interdependence and *interconnectedness* also relate to the primacy of the collective as each individual understands that it 'makes sense' to care for one another. Schmid similarly emphasises the importance of seeing the 'interconnections' [Zusammenhänge] in the world. While he does not explain the interdependence of human life with that of other creatures, he explains that only through understanding and awareness of how aspects of life and in the world interconnect, and how our actions and interventions affect other aspects and other people in our environment, which then again reflect back on us, can we actively shape our life and take effective action. For this, a combination of *Bildung* [self-formation; self-cultivation] and practical wisdom is needed. The link to *buen vivir* here would be that our understanding of how our actions impact on our local and global environment, for example, in the form of global warming but also mass extinction of animals and plant populations, will at some point affect the quality of life for ourselves or our children and next generations. Provided that we care for our offsprings, if we have them, and the continued existence of the human species overall, and their ability to live well instead of having to struggle to survive – again, *phronésis* is the driving faculty for these considerations – one will have to moderate one's actions in line with what is good for all rather than only with what is good for oneself. A notion that is also reflected in Biesta's (2022) approach to world-centred education, as will be discussed in the later chapters of this book.

Māori Worldviews and the Art of Living[8]

Beyond the Latin American concept of *buen vivir* and the underlying indigenous traditions, I want to also comment briefly on similarities and differences between Schmid's art of living philosophy and the indigenous worldview of Māori people in Aotearoa New Zealand. It needs to be noted here that, similar to the indigenous peoples of Latin America, there is no one coherent worldview of Māori. Māori people in Aotearoa New Zealand are organised in tribes, so called *iwi*, and sub-tribes – *hapū*. Each *iwi* and hapū hold their own

---

8 I want to acknowledge the work Ayo Palmer has made as research assistant in the context of linking Māori worldviews and frameworks to Schmid's art of living, and my colleague Te Hurinui Karaka-Clarke, who co-leads this particular research project with me.

THE ART OF LIVING FOR INDIVIDUAL AND COMMUNITY GOOD   45

traditions, practices, and worldviews. However, it is probably fair to say that, similar to the different indigenous peoples of Latin America, Māori across iwi and hapū share some common values and a common base understanding of viewing the world and the place of people and community within it. These include, among others, the value of *whanaungatanga*[9] [relationships and connections with others], *manaakitanga* [hospitality and care], *whakapapa* [genealogy and connection to one's ancestry and place], *tika* [right, correct], *pono* [integrity, fairness] and *aroha* [compassion, care], *Tine Rangatiratanga* [self-determination], as well as the emphasis on the collective, and the importance of land and place – *whenua* (cf. Tate, 2012; Savage et al., 2014).

While a detailed evaluation and comparison between Māori concepts and worldviews[10] and Schmid's art of living is still under way, I would like to highlight some preliminary similarities and differences that emerged in work undertaken so far. In the following, I will briefly discuss some of the key themes that were identified so far.

Agency and self-determination are expresses across all reviewed indigenous frameworks and reflects the importance placed on shaping one's own – and the collective's for that matter – path rather than being driven or defined by external regimes, links to Schmid's active approach to taking responsibility for one's own life and actions. As such, Māori worldview and Schmid's philosophy find common ground in the active element of engaging with life and taking responsibility for one's own life and being in the world. A difference of view in this context, however, is that in Māoridom, self-determination is often linked to self-determination of iwi and hapū about their own affairs. As such, it is an ongoing contentious point that derived from conflicting translations of *Te Tiriti o Waitangi* [The Treaty of Waitangi][11]. So, while Schmid's

---

9   The suggested translations for Māori terms and concepts are indicative of meaning only. While commonly used in Aotearoa New Zealand, these English translations capture only parts of the complex meaning behind the listed concepts.

10 In our work so far, we focused on seven indigenous frameworks and key sources: Te Wa (Tate 2012), Te Wheke (Pere, Nicholson and Zealand 1997), Mana Wahine (Pihama 2020), Mauri Ora (Alsop and Kupenga 2016), Manaaki Tāngata – A conceptual framework of happiness (McDonald 2016), Māori perspective of flourishing whānau (Rolleston, McDonald and Miskelly 2021), and Aroha (Elder 2020).

11 Te tiriti o Waitangi is the founding historical document in which many Māori chieftains allowed the British Crown to establish a governing entity in Aotearoa New Zealand that was intended to oversee the relations between indigenous Māori and (mostly) British settlers. The then signed version in Te Reo Māori [Māori language], however, showed

model focuses solely on the agency of the individual, in the Māori frameworks both the individual and the collective are considered in relation to agency and especially self-determination.

Living with pain and negative emotions is considered in both accounts. In Schmid's philosophy, the experience of pain and suffering can serve as incentive to take up responsibility for one's own life, develop agency, and shape one's life actively. As such, pain and negative emotions are not something to be avoided but seen as something that can support personal growths and development. Similarly, McDonald (2016) and Rolleston et al. (2021) comment on the role hardship plays for their concepts of happiness and success in Māori contexts. Rolleston et al. particularly reconceptualise happiness not as the absence of hardship and suffering, but the capacity and ability to overcome it. As such, clear links between Schmid's philosophy and Māori frameworks can be identified.

The Relationship between self, collective and environment stands out as both showing similarities and differences alike. In Schmid's ethics of practical wisdom, as discussed above, the reciprocal relationship between oneself, others and the environment is explained as important to care for oneself and the development of one's own art of living. Similarly, across the reviewed Māori frameworks, the reciprocity between people and nature and the responsibility Māori people have to look after the environment as the stewards of their ancestral lands is highlighted. What differs, however, is – similar to the discussion in the context of the indigenous peoples of Latin Amerika – the emphasis that is given to each of these entities. In Māoridom, the connection with the natural environment and the collective is emphasised to the point where it shapes and blends the lines between self, collective and land [whenua]. Schmid, on the other hand, taking a traditionally more Western approach suggests expanding circles of care that place the individual at the centre, followed by people and environment as distinct entities in which one stands in relationship with rather than being part of one's self and identity.

differences in wording to the English version accompanying the Māori version, which, among others, contributed to a long and ongoing dispute between Māori and the New Zealand government about Māori rights, protections and other matters. The full complexity of the matter cannot be discussed here, but mention of this background seems helpful to understand some of the finer points of differences mentioned in the text.

Self-reflection and self-mastery emerged as a shared theme between Schmid's philosophy and reviewed Māori frameworks. While Schmid emphasises (self-) reflection as key to cultivate an art of living and ethics of friendship and engagement with others, in the reviewed Māori frameworks, the notion of self-mastery came to the fore as something that seems to capture a similar notion in relation to self. Alsop and Kupenga's (2016) Mauri Ora framework references whakahautanga [self-mastery] as crucial for wisdom, making meaning, and self-direction. Elder's (2020) guide to writing a whakatauki [significant saying; proverb] also requires the capacity for self-reflection, asking the reader to reflect not only on their experiences, emotions, and surroundings, but on their instincts. Similarly for Schmid, the 'reflective element' of the art of living encompasses personal norms, values, and beliefs, one's actions and habits, as well as the ability to critically reflect on the wider context of one's surroundings to see the interconnections in the world, as commented on earlier.

As a final point, *the importance of time* shall be mentioned here. For Schmid, it is particularly the future and cultivating a care for the future and future generations that requires consideration beyond the immediate under the ethics of practical wisdom. While Schmid considers the past as relevant as so far that it helps to understand the present and the interconnections in the world, it does not seem to receive any further emphasis beyond this function. In Māoridom, consideration of the future for the wellbeing of the collective is similarly important, but so is the emphasis on the importance of the past and the links to ancestry. Whakapapa [genealogy] plays an important role for Māori identity and sense of belonging and place in the world from which meaning is derived. Both Pihama (2020) and Pere et al. (1997) discuss the importance of finding one's roots to manifest one's journey and direction in life.

Implications for Education Regarding Individual and Community Good

What emerges from these contemplations and links between Schmid's philosophy – and particularly his ethics of practical wisdom – and indigenous, collectivist approaches to seeing and engaging with the world, is a strong indication that community good and individual good are interconnected and that the wellbeing, so to say, of the community lies in the best interest of each individual. It also suggests, though, that the development of an art of living for its members can lie in the best interest of the community. That similar values, although approached from opposite directions, are evident in Schmid's ethics of practical wisdom, based on Western philosophical traditions and approached from an individualistic starting point, as well as in indigenous worldviews that prioritise the collective and community good as the foundation for ethical human actions suggests this reciprocal relationship between individual and community good as a possible universal reality of the human condition. As such, Schmid's concept of the art of living might offer a bridge between different cultural contexts as well as a counter, similar to buen vivir and the reviewed Māori frameworks and values, to current dominant cultural norms, values and beliefs of self-maximisation, consumerism and unchecked egoism, as arguably promoted by neoliberal ideology (cf. McDonald et al., 2017). Therefore, through people engaging in and developing their own art of living, including their strengthening of prudence and practical wisdom in the process, it is conceivable that individuals would not only shape their own lives towards what they perceive a beautiful life to be, but also support the development of an environment that supports all members of a community, and therefore the community as a whole, to live more 'beautifully'.

Two questions arise, however: (i) how does an environment supportive of the development of an art of living for everyone might look like, and (ii) what does it mean for the good of a community or society that is structured in such manner. Responding to (i), I would argue that such an environment does not have to stray far from what many societies strive towards and value already – at least in theory, although how values are realised and are guiding people's action might shift to some extent. One key aspect for an art of living supporting environment would be lived *tolerance for other ways of being and living in the world*: the acceptance that different people pursue different life pathways, not just in term of their job pursuit, but also their approach to relationships, ways of living, and cultural diversity as it is expressed in any noticeable way. This is not to say that we should give in to relativism or nihilism in regard to moral values. The argument has been made above that to develop an art of living, as understood here, includes and requires the development of an ethics of practical wisdom, which sets reasonable limitations for one's own actions and the freedom one claims for oneself but also grants others. However, one needs to ask oneself if the foreign practice one observes, which sits outside of what one might have experienced in one's own cultural setting, is contrary to the fundamental values one holds dear, or maybe just a bit different from the experienced norm but still well acceptable considering one's own held fundamental values[12]. An awareness for our human disposition to frown upon and be 'afraid' of the unfamiliar, as well as an awareness for our tendency to group people as either 'one of us' or 'not one of us' will help to uphold a reasonable level of tolerance, while maintaining one's ability to critically reflect and take reasonable action when a situation arises that is contrary to one's fundamental values. An example to illustrate this would be the experience of family violence. One's tolerance for how other people organise their personal relationships – including how different genders relate to each other and show respect to each other in different cultural context, as long as they are mutually agreed on and entered freely into by all partners, which aligns with the assumed fundamental value of freedom – does not extend to relationships where one partner is subjugated to violence that would limit their freedom and their right to a dignified human life, and effect their ability to pursue their own art of living. Again, the faculty of prudence and practical wisdom will be helpful to see the boundaries between tolerance towards other ways of being and unacceptable ways of behaviour.

In conjunction with tolerance towards other ways of being, an art of living supportive environment would include community members *to refrain from a dogmatic proclamation of values, norms, and beliefs*. While the right to express one's views and position would certainly be included under the aspect of tolerance, along with reasonable arguments for one's position in relevant circumstances, members of a community supporting the development of people's personal art of living should refrain from claiming authority about the 'truth' of moral values or any 'right' way of living or doing things. An acceptance of plurality of perspectives and a public discourse that discusses reasonably and respectfully the implications and complexities of different positions but not diminishes other positions out of principle would likely feature in such an environment. This links with a general expectation of *respectful reciprocal*

---

12 I distinguish here between fundamental (or maybe foundational) values that a person sees as integral to their character and being in the world and non-fundamental values or expressions that would, arguably, sit closer to norms rather than values in a strict sense. Examples of fundamental values might be freedom (in its various forms and complexities), tolerance, honesty, or the right to a humane and dignified life. A non-fundamental value that more aligns with personal or cultural norms might be donating to charitable causes, pursuing monogamous relationships, healthy eating habits, or punctuality. – Unfortunately, I must only glance over a host of complexities in this context of moral ethics here, which sits outside of the scope and focus of this chapter and book, but which I plan to expand on in future work.

engagement with others in such an environment. To uphold the dignity of every human being one engages with and to treat them respectfully to the best of one's understanding of the complexities of norms and cultural rules in play between oneself and the other[13]. Another aspect already mentioned above is the *freedom* to act and choose within reason as discussed above. This 'freedom to', however, is contingent on certain 'freedoms from', such as freedom from deprivation and poverty, freedom from oppression, and freedom from a struggle for survival. While I would argue that the development of an art of living is not an elitist model for the rich and powerful, it certainly depends on basic human needs for survival being met for the individual to be able to direct thought and energy towards what a beautiful life might look like, rather than to struggle for mere survival.

So far, none of the aspects mentioned proclaim anything fundamentally new or different to how most democratic societies are structured – at least in theory. However, a society that values the development of an art of living might be able to make stronger inroads towards some of these aspirations, such as lived tolerance and a more reflective approach to one's own actions and engagement with others. Possibly more authenticity and alignment between held values, norms and beliefs and one's own actions might be enacted through the development of one's own art of living. What can be observed currently are conflicting values and norms that lead to societal challenges and hardship for people in many societies today. For example, I would argue that most people would support the idea that every child should have the opportunity to grow up and live a dignified human life with basic needs for survival being met, and potentially a shot at 'happiness'. This belief and associated values have underpinned the social welfare state model of the mid-20th century. However, some of the values, norms and beliefs that are supported by proponents of capitalism and especially in the context of neoliberalism since the 1970s and 1980s to today are in conflict with these values and have, although partly responsible and supportive of technological growths and other positive developments, led to societies that are marked by extreme inequality in terms of distribution of wealth and resources, inequality of opportunities, a decline in the relative income for many (especially the lower 50% income earners in many Western

---

13 I want to acknowledge here that while respectful or dignified behaviour towards others might be conceived as a fundamental value and a desirable trait in an art of living supportive environment, the perception of what actions constitute respect for others are culturally contextual and need to be negotiated appropriately. Again, an attitude of tolerance towards the other can bridge differences in conceptions of respectful behaviour and actions.

countries) and the continuation of a struggle for survival for large parts of the world population, not just in the so called 'Global South' but increasingly in countries of the 'Global North' as well[14]. A society in which the development of *phronésis* is supported and the development of each person's art of living is valued, such conflicts between values, norms, beliefs, and actions might be seen as problematic and acted on by the majority of its members which might lead to actual social change and increased equity, as discussed further below.

Another aspect that might go beyond current social norms and arrangements, however, would be the *reciprocal support to develop key faculties relevant for an art of living*. A social environment supportive in this manner would provide opportunities for people to develop faculties like critical (self-)reflection, prudence and practical wisdom, open-mindedness and tolerance, caring and creative thinking, as well as the exposure to relevant areas of (life-)knowledge that allows individuals to consider and reflect on how they want to live and how a beautiful life for them might look like. These opportunities can manifest in various ways. It can be embedded in parental (and communal) upbringing and raising of children, it can be embedded in everyday encounters, for example, by living and practicing these faculties in an observable manner that allows others to pick up on them and develop their own abilities. And it can be embedded in intentional education contexts, such as the compulsory education system but also other non-compulsory educational settings. How this can be implemented in schools and curricula will be discussed further in Chapters Five and Six.

At this point, the reader might remember that I indicated two questions that emerged from the discussion above: (i) how an art of living supportive environment might look like, and (ii) what that might mean for the 'good' of society. Turning now to the second questions, I would argue that a society providing a supportive environment for the development of an art of living for all people, including an education system that is organised and oriented towards such an end, could conceivably become a more equitable and just society than what has emerged under current neoliberal structures. As the focus of such a social environment would move away from mainly amassing wealth and standing towards a plurality of life aims, members of such a society would likely be open to a more equitable distribution of resources that allow each individual to pursue their own approach to a beautiful life. This might include a social welfare structure that provides a universal basic income, or

---

14 See, for example, stats on inequality.org: https://inequality.org/facts/global-inequality/

at least a societal participation income[15], for each member, and likely a tax system that shifts the distribution of burden more fairly towards the 'haves' rather than the 'have nots'. This idea, again, is not new but would, I argue, be more acceptable to and supported by a society that supports their members in the development of their own art of living rather than be driven by current ideologies we see in neoliberal, capitalist national environments[16].

Going along with a more equitable distribution of wealth and resources would be a more equitable distribution and value of income for work rendered. It is difficult for me, and many others I would argue, to understand why certain positions in our economy and industry attract income that is hundreds, sometimes thousand times higher than what the lowest paid workers in any given organisation receive. While monetary incentives for certain jobs might be a necessity, and there are differences in burdens (physical, emotional, mental, or otherwise) between jobs that would be fair to compensate for through reasonable income differences, the extent of these differences in many current settings seems disproportionate and unjust (cf. Brown et al., 2020). While the scope of this book does not allow a detailed discussion of the complexity of this and related issues, real world examples can be found in, for example, Scandinavian societies that seem to have a much more reasonable distribution of income as well as the value associated with the work undertaken in various jobs and professions. Considering the current challenges of the gross undervalue in social standing and monetary compensation for system critical jobs such as workers in the food industry, health system, and education system, to name only some that could largely be group under 'essential services' that has come to the fore during the COVID-19 pandemic, one wonders how more equitable societies have fared in these situations. Even though New Zealand has weathered the pandemic fairly well, in the aftermath we have seen systems at the breaking point due to underfunding and the ongoing lack of appropriate social and financial recognition of these professions.

Beyond a more equitable distribution of wealth and resources, the idea of *equal educational opportunity* would likely see much stronger commitment and

---

15 For more details, the proceedings of a symposium discussing the pros and cons of participant income vs. universal income is introduced by Stirton (2018).
16 This is not to say that every aspect of neoliberalism nor capitalism is bad; however, I would argue that the pendulum has swung too far in one direction and in aspects of our social structures and social consciousness, we have lost the view on what is reasonable, desirable and proper for the thriving and flourishing of human people, not just economies (cf. Brown, Lauder & Cheung, 2020; and Cornali and Federica 2022 for a critique).

possibly a revised focus, as will be discussed in more detail in the following chapter. Current persistent inequities, despite the best intentions and efforts by many teachers, principals, academics and others in education systems, might finally be addressed on a more fundamental level when the neoliberally driven circumstances of accountability, performativity and marketisation of education focused on job-readiness and economic advancement take a backseat, or at least are balanced with other equally important values and purposes of education (Nairn, Sligo & Higgins, 2012; Biesta, 2015; Keddie, 2016). Efforts in schooling and the (compulsory) education system could then refocus on what is important and involved for each young generation to live well as holistic human beings (rather than mainly contributors to industry and economy) – to develop their own art of living and pursue a beautiful life. How education under such focus and aim might look like will be considered further in the later chapters of this book.

Conclusion

In this chapter, I have discussed the challenges and complexity of the notion of 'good' in relation to the individual and society. Schmid's terminology of a 'beautiful life' and his individual based approach to the art of living has been reiterated as one way to address the challenges and preconceptions of how a 'good life' could be, and often is, understood. I have further outlined the challenge that could be laid against Schmid's somewhat subjectivist notion of a beautiful life being a question of individual taste by discussing the ethics of the art of living based on Aristotle's notion of *phronésis* and the resulting expanding *circles of care* that start with the care of the self and expand into a care for others, a care for society and humanity, and a care for the environment and our planet. Through the *ethics of practical wisdom*, it was argued, the individual will come to transform their inherent egoistic self-interest into a form of *enlightened self-interest*, understanding that an environment – social and otherwise – that is conducive to the development of people's art of living and pursuit of a beautiful life will also support their own aspirations in this matter.

Acknowledging, however, that Schmid's philosophy – while eclectic and drawing on many stands of philosophy – has been developed in a Central European cultural context and is based on, what can be considered, traditional Western philosophy, I explored how Schmid's art of living concept relates to two indigenous concepts and worldviews: the concept of *buen vivir* from the

South Americas, and the worldview of Māori from Aotearoa New Zealand. While many differences exist between Schmid's philosophical approach and cultural concepts based on the traditions on various indigenous peoples in Latin America and in Aotearoa New Zealand respectively, we were able to establish links in regard to what it might mean to live well, the complexity and variability of human pathways, values, norms and beliefs, and – most notably – in the levels of care that underpin human moral behaviour across the examined indigenous traditions as well as Schmid's ethics of the art of living as derived through the faculty of prudence and practical wisdom. The notable difference being the approach to these ethical principles: Schmid's ethical model is based on the centrality of the individual, whereas the indigenous traditions reviewed here emphasised the centrality of nature (the planet) followed by the community and finally the individual. As such, while the cultural approaches have what could be seen as detrimentally opposed starting positions, they arrive at similar layers or circles of care that can lead to similar ethical decision making despite the vastly different cultural context and traditions they developed under. Therefore, I argued that Schmid's art of living model could be seen as one approach or bridge that can span the divide between cultures focusing on the individual and cultures that emphasis communal ways of being.

Leaning on this bridge, I have argued that an interrelation of the individual good and the good or 'wellbeing' of a community or society might be a universal (or close to) human condition. From here, I have argued then that Schmid's art of living can be seen as a reasonable approach to not only further individual good through the development of each individual's own art of living and pursuit of a beautiful life, but also social and societal good through the care each individual (if engaged in the art of living) will come to express for the people and environment around them. Reciprocally, I have argued that it is equally in the interest of a society to support the development of each person's own art of living. Hence, the art of living for each individual has been positioned as a means to societal good and should consequently become a guiding principle for a societal setup that provides an environment that is conducive to the development of the art of living for all its members.

I have finally outlined how such an art of living supportive environment might look like, what aspects and characteristics it might have, and I have suggested principles that might govern the interaction between people. Among others, *equity* and *equal educational opportunity* were proposed as two characteristics of such a social structure. In the next chapter, I will argue how equal educational opportunity might be understood through an art of living lens and the implications following for an education system based on the aim to provide equal opportunity for students to develop their own art of living.

Acknowledgements

This chapter incorporates material, with permission, from a previous book chapter 'Education towards a beautiful life in an imperfect world', published by Peter Lang in Kamp et al. (eds), 2023, *Wellbeing – Global Policies and Perspectives. Insights from Aotearoa New Zealand and beyond*.

This chapter was also informed by and contains substantial material in edited form from work previously published in the *Journal of the Canadian Philosophy of Education Society, Philosophical Inquiry in Education* with permission: Teschers, C., & Nieto, M. (2023). Buen Vivir and the Art of living: Comparing Western and Latin American perspectives on living a 'good life', *PIE*, 30(3), 207–220.

References

Alsop, P., & Kupenga, T. R. (2016). *Mauri ora: wisdom from the Māori world*. Nelson, New Zealand: Potton & Burton.

Aristotle. (1996). *The Nicomachean ethics*. Edited by T. Griffith. London, England: Wordsworth Editions Limited.

Bieri, P. (2006). *Das Handwerk der Freiheit: Über die Entdeckung des eigenen Willens*. Frankfurt, Germany: Fischer Verlag.

Biesta, G. (2013). *The beautiful risk of education*. Paradigm.

Biesta, G. (2022). *World-centred education: A view for the present*. Routledge.

Biesta, G. J. J. (2015). Good education in an age of measurement: Ethics, politics, democracy, *Good Education in an Age of Measurement: Ethics, Politics, Democracy*. doi:10.4324/9781315634319.

Boniwell, I. (2008). *Positive psychology in a nutshell*. London, England: PWBC.

Brown, P., Lauder, H., & Cheung, S. Y. (2020). *The death of Human Capital?, The death of Human Capital?: Its failed promise and how to renew it in an age of disruption*. Oxford University Press. doi:10.1093/oso/9780190644307.001.0001.

Burgos, A. (2016). Buen Vivir con la naturaleza en las instituciones educativas: Una necesidad en Boyacá, Colombia. *Culturales Época*, 4(2), 185–208.

Cornali and Federica. (2022). Human capital to come. Death and rebirth of a theory?. http://journals.openedition.org/qds, (89–LXVI), 151–160. doi:10.4000/QDS.5011.

Durán López, M. (2010). Sumak Kawsay o Buen Vivir, desde la cosmovisión andina hacia la ética de la sustentabilidad. *Pensamiento Actual*, 10(14–15), 5161.

Elder, H. (2020). *Aroha: Māori wisdom for a contented life lived in harmony with our planet.* Auckland: Penguin Random House New Zealand. Available at: https://go.exlibris.link/LWFQftGh.

Esteva, G. (2011). Más allá del desarrollo: la buena vida. *América Latina en Movimiento,* 23(2), 1–5.

Feldman, F. (2004). *Pleasure and the good life: Concerning the nature, varieties and plausibility of hedonism.* New York, NY: Clarendon.

Foucault, M. (1984). *The care of the self.* London, England: Penguin Books (The history of sexuality).

Houtart, F. (2011). El concepto de sumak kawsay (buen vivir) y su correspondencia con el bien común de la humanidad. *Revista de Filosofía,* 69(3), 7–33.

Keddie, A. (2016). Children of the market: Performativity, neoliberal responsibilisation and the construction of student identities. *Oxford Review of Education,* 42(1), 108–122. doi:10.1080/03054985.2016.1142865.

Kowii, A. (2015). El sumak kawsay. *La Macchina Sognante* [Preprint]. Available at: http://www.lamacchinasognante.com/il-sumak-kawsay/ (Accessed: 8 May 2024).

Kraut, R. (2010). Aristotle's ethics. In E. N. Zalta (Ed.), *The Stanford encyclopedia of philosophy.* Available at: http://plato.stanford.edu/archives/sum2010/entries/aristotle-ethics/.

Kristjánsson, K. (2012). Positive psychology and positive education: Old wine in new bottles?. *Educational Psychologist,* 47(2), 86–105. doi:10.1080/00461520.2011.610678.

McDonald, M. (2016). 'Manaaki Tāngata – The secret to happiness: Narratives from Older Māori in the Bay of Plenty'. Available at: https://researchspace.auckland.ac.nz/handle/2292/31981 (Accessed: 14 August 2023).

McDonald, M. et al. (2017). Social psychology, consumer culture and neoliberal political economy. *Journal for the Theory of Social Behaviour,* 47(3), 363–379. Available at: https://search.ebscohost.com/login.aspx?direct=true&AuthType=shib&db=sih&AN=124970056&site=ehost-live&custid=s1165276.

Medina, J. (2001). *Suma qamaña la comprensión indígena de la vida Buena.* PADEP/GTZ.

Medina, J. (2006). *Suma qamaña: Por una convivialidad postindustrial.* Garza Azul Editores.

Nairn, K. M., Sligo, J., & Higgins, J. (2012). *Children of Rogernomics : A neoliberal generation leaves school.* Dunedin, N.Z.: Otago University Press.

Pere, R. R., Nicholson, N., & Zealand, A. A. L. N. (1997). *Te wheke: A celebration of infinite wisdom* (2nd ed.). Gisborne, N.Z.: Ao Ako Global Learning New Zealand. Available at: https://go.exlibris.link/gXkmNKGy.

Pihama, L. (2020). Mana Wahine: Decolonising Gender in Aotearoa. *Australian Feminist Studies,* 35(106), 351–365. Available at: https://search.ebscohost.com/login.aspx?direct=true&AuthType=shib&db=sih&AN=151044942&site=ehost-live&custid=s1165276.

Prage, L. (2015). Lekil Kuxlejal – An alternative to development? A field study in Chiapas, Mexico. Available at: http://lup.lub.lu.se/student-papers/record/7857560 (Accessed: 24 March 2023).

Quijano, O. (2012). *Ecosimías: Visiones y prácticas de diferencia económico/cultural en contextos de multiplicidad.* Editorial Universidad del Cauca.

Rico, C. (2019). Reflexiones sobre el buen vivir y el cuidado de la casa común: Comunicación y diálogos entre perspectivas coloniales, pos- y de coloniales sobre el desarrollo. In J. Pereira (Ed.), *Buen vivir, cuidado de la casa común y reconciliación* (pp. 47–65). Editorial Pontificia Universidad Javeriana. Available at: https://www.javeriana.edu.co/unesco/pdf/LibroCatedraUNESCO.pdf (Accessed: 8 May 2024).

Roberts, P. (2016). *Happiness, hope, and despair: Rethinking the role of education.* Peter Lang.

Rolleston, A., McDonald, M., & Miskelly, P. (2021). Our story: A Māori perspective of flourishing whānau. doi:10.1080/1177083X.2021.1981955.

Savage, C. et al. (2014). Huakina mai: A kaupapa Māori approach to relationship and behaviour support. *Australian Journal of Indigenous Education, 43*(2), 165–174. doi:10.1017/jie.2014.23.

Schmid, W. (2000a). *Auf der Suche nach einer neuen Lebenskunst.* Frankfurt, Germany: Suhrkamp.

Schmid, W. (2000b) *Philosophie der Lebenskunst: Eine Grundlegung.* Frankfurt: Suhrkamp.

Seligman, M. E. P. (2011). *Flourish: A visionary new understanding of happiness and well-being.* New York, NY: Free Press.

Stirton, L. (2018). Symposium introduction: Anthony Atkinson's "The Case for a Participation Income". *Political Quarterly, 89*(2), 254–255. Available at: https://search.ebscohost.com/login.aspx?direct=true&AuthType=shib&db=poh&AN=129935007&site=ehost-live&custid=s1165276.

Tate, H. (2012). *He puna iti i te ao mārama: A little spring in the world of light.* Auckland, N.Z: Libro International. Available at: https://go.exlibris.link/jd3dDrWD.

Teschers, C. (2018). *Education and Schmid's art of living, Education and Schmid's art of living.* Routledge. doi:10.4324/9781315563848.

Teschers, C. (2023). Education towards a beautiful life. In Kamp, A., Brown, C., O'Toole, V., & McMenamin, T. (eds.). *Wellbeing: Global Policies and Perspectives.* Peter Lang.

Teschers, C., & Nieto, M. (2023). Buen Vivir and the art of living: Comparing Western and Latin American perspectives on living a "Good Life". *Philosophical Inquiry in Education, 30*(3), 207–220. Available at: https://www.oecdbetterlifeindex.org/topics/life-satisfaction.

Tortosa, J. M. (2009). Sumak kawsay, suma qamaña, buen vivir. *Fundación Carolina-España* [Preprint]. Available at: https://base.socioeco.org/docs/_bitstream_10644_2789_1_raa-28_20mar_c3_ada_20tortosa_2c_20sumak_20kawasay_2c_20suma_20qama_c3_b1a_2c_20buen_20vivir.pdf (Accessed: 8 May 2024).

Viasus, L., Posada, A., & Díaz, H. (2016). Ordenando el territorio: Entre el camino de los ancestros y la perspectiva contemporánea. Caso comunidad indígena muisca de Bosa, Bogotá-Colombia. *Prospectiva. Revista de Trabajo Social e Intervencion Social, 22*, 141–171.

Vidal, W. E., & O'Steen, B. (2023). What counts as wellbeing?. In A. Kamp et al. (Eds.), *Wellbeing. Global policies and perspectives* (pp. 11–34). Peter Lang.

· 4 ·

EQUITY AND 'EQUAL EDUCATIONAL OPPORTUNITY' FOR A BEAUTIFUL LIFE

In this chapter, I argue for a different take on equal educational opportunity that deviates somewhat from common positions but might offer a pathway to overcome some of the challenges pertinent in the debate to date, potentially providing a bridge between positions of outcome equality versus adequacy in education. To do this, I provide an overview of the complexity of the equity debate in education in Part 1 of this chapter, followed by proposing an art of living approach to equal educational opportunity in Part 2, that makes suggestions how equity in education can reasonably and meaningfully be addressed, as well as potentially make a contribution to equity and equality in society.

Introduction

Much has been written about equity and equality in society and education, often focusing on either a just distribution of resources, or on an equitable approach to education that arguably allows for equal social, occupational, and economic opportunities in adult life through education (Peters, 1966; Coleman, 1975; Bowles & Gintis, 1976; Rawls, 2001; Brighouse, 2003, 2014; Shields, Newman & Satz, 2023). The question of equity and social justice is also key in the debate of diversity and inclusion (e.g., Bevan-Brown, 2006; Ballard, 2012), as unequal distribution of resources and opportunities often accompany circumstances in which diversity and difference can lead to disability within society and education. To tackle these inequalities, education is often tasked to generate equal social and economic opportunities for all towards a just and inclusive society (Coleman, 1975; Ainscow, 2012; Brighouse, 2014). However, considering the fact that each education system is operating within local social and cultural constrains, education more often than not fails to achieve this high challenge (cf. Bowles & Gintis, 1976, 2002). In contrast, if following a holistic art of living approach to education that considers each person as a unique human being, embraces diversity from a broad perspective, and places the personal development of each individual and his or her ability to live a good and beautiful life in the foreground, the notions of equity and equality can be approached from a different angle – for both education and society.

It is a simple fact that inequality in life is inevitable: experiences, aspirations, interests, skills, possessions, opportunities, etc., are diverse and no two people *are* the same or *have* the same. This diversity, however, should not be considered as 'bad', it just reflects the uniqueness of each human being. Hardly anyone would argue that all human beings should be made the same, i.e., made to have the same experiences, same interests, and same aspirations, develop the same skills and possess the same items (cf. Gosepath, 2021). Such an approach would violate all conceptions of personal freedom and individual flourishing, and it would most likely lead to a society that is at least monotonous and boring, if not impossible to survive on any level beyond the most rudimentary farming community utilising handmade tools.

So why do I start with this rather obvious, and partly flawed ('equality' is not necessarily synonymous to 'sameness') observation? It is to start with a questioning approach towards the notions of (in-)equality, equity, fairness and justice. In this chapter, I will reflect on some of the challenges of the debate around social justice, and especially equality, equity and equal educational opportunity, resulting from differences in understanding of the meaning of these terms and the context they are applied to. Hence, the first part of this chapter will explore and summarise aspects of the discourse of social and educational justice to clarify relevant terminology and address conflicting positions, and to identify some of the key issues to justice and fairness in the social and educational debate. In the second part of this article, I will then introduce a different approach towards equity in education, what I will then refer to as *equal educational opportunity*, drawing on the philosophical concept of the art of living (Schmid, 2000). This different approach is then explored in relation to social justice, diversity and the concept of inclusion in education and society.

Exploring Equality, Equity, Justice, and Fairness in Relation to Education

One of the challenges in the debate around *(in-)equality in education* is the transfer of the term 'equality' from other discourses, such as the social justice or the economic in-equality debate, to education: for example, the 'simple' meaning of equal distribution of resources among members of society (Gosepath, 2021). Terms, such as 'income inequality,' 'economic inequality,' and 'social inequality' generally refer to an unequal distribution of money, assets and positionality between members of society (cf. Institute for Policy Studies, 2023; Shields et al., 2023). What comes implicitly with this monetary inequality, but is not always made explicit, is the result of *unequal opportunities* for health, housing, food, jobs, lifestyle, personal development, education, life expectancy, and many more, including a potentially reduced capacity to actively and informed exercise one's rights as democratic citizen of a country (Institute for Policy Studies, 2023; Shields et al., 2023). Hence, the argument in the context of the *general equality* debate states that unequal distribution of resources leads to unequal opportunities in life. However, transferring this understanding of 'equality' directly to education is problematic, as will be discussed below[1].

To complicate this relationship, and to bridge the gap to equality in education, we need to consider that not all people are the same. This point has been advanced especially in the context of social justice and inclusion of people with impairments: people are different and have different abilities; therefore, they need different resources for similar opportunities. However, it also extends to other areas of diversity, such as cultural background, gender, age, etc. Despite the currency of this issue, it is not a new insight at all: Aristotle (2002, 1131a-1131b) already stated that justice demands that people who are equal are treated equally, and people who are unequal are receiving unequal

---

1 Sigfried Uhl (2001) discusses the challenges of transferring terminology from other disciplines and discourses to education, pointing out that a rigorous definition of how these terms are to be understood and used in education is often lacking. The meaning of the transferred terms is often changing in the educational debate, leading to confusion and a range of meanings across discourses and disciplines which leads to misunderstandings and is not conducive to a clear academic debate. See also Gosepath (2021).

distribution. Hence, with an eye on *equal opportunities* in the reading of fairness and justice (cf. Rawls, 2001; Gosepath, 2021), a certain unequal distribution of resources is justified if it leads to more equal 'opportunities' in life. However, what these opportunities are is not always explicit or clear. One approach that can shed some light on this issue is the 'equal rights' discourse in the inclusion debate, advocating that people with 'disabilities'[2] have the same rights as not 'disabled' people, such as a right to work, access to all public spaces, use of public facilities (transport, places, etc.), equal rights to education, fulfilment of life, etc. The argument extends similarly to other forms of diversity, as mentioned before.

What has been touched on in the discussion above, but warrants more explanation, is the meaning of the notions of 'fairness' and 'justice' in relation to equality. These terms have been shaped strongly by Rawls (2001) and his famous thought experiment of 'the veil of ignorance'. According to Rawls, if we imagine a society, and we do not know where in this society we would be placed once it comes into being, people would generally opt for a society in which resources are distributed as equally as possible, and that unequal distributions of resources are linked to special circumstances, such as to compensate for the challenges of impairments, or to offset the added responsibility of certain positions within society. However, access to these positions needs to be available to all in principle, and the selection processes need to be fair. Such a society would then be considered by many, according to Rawls, as 'just' or 'fair'[3]. Therefore, the notions of justice and fairness, I would argue, constitute a higher concept that subsumes the idea of equal distribution of resources, to compensate for differences in a diverse population[4].

---

2   The understanding and definition of 'disability' is contested and shifting over time; where it has been understood as a negative attribute, a medical condition, of an individual historically, it is more recently seen, through the lens of social constructivism, as an effect of a socially constructed environment that is disabling for some people based on diverse abilities rather than inherent shortcomings of individuals or groups of people.
3   Rawls and others have expanded on this argument and a more nuanced account is presented, for example, in Shields et al. (2023).
4   An extensive body of literature exists concerning social justice and equality and shall not be repeated here. Good summaries have been provided, for example, by Gosepath (2021), Miller (2017), and Shields et al. (2023).

Equality and Education

If we now apply these terms of the social-justice debate to education, a similar challenge arises: in which frame of reference do we use the term equality? Do we apply equality towards (i) equal access to education, (ii) an equal distribution of resources within education to support students, or do we apply equality towards (iii) educational outcomes after a certain period of schooling?[5] If we focus on an equal distribution of resources in education alone (as in ii), equality is used in a rather flat understanding that in effect continues and, according to Bowles and Gintis (2002), even promotes socio-economic inequality, and, hence, is rather unjust. To counter this flat understanding of equal distribution of educational resources, some authors have suggested the term *equity* (e.g., Peters, 1966) in education, which closely links to the notion of 'justice,' as used by Rawls (2001), and is mainly directed towards educational outcome, also referred to as *equal educational opportunity*, or 'equal adult opportunities' by Coleman (1975: 28). However, similar to equality in education, 'equal educational opportunity' can be applied to different frames of reference as outlined above; it can be understood (a) as equal opportunity to *access* education, or (b) as equal *outcome* opportunities, which reflects the reading proposed by Coleman as 'equal adult opportunities'. But again, Coleman does not state clearly what is meant by that, merely referring to 'occupation and otherwise' (p. 28), not clarifying what these other opportunities might be. Satz (2007) proposes citizenship as a broad concept of educational outcome that should be reached by all as a minimal standard for *adequacy* in education, whereas White (2011) defends a form of personal wellbeing and flourishing as this 'otherwise'. In the second part of this chapter, I will argue another possible approach towards clarifying this 'otherwise' of opportunities, which links with White's argument, but also deviates in some respect.

However, first, I would like to finalise this exploration of terminology in the debate for a shared understanding of how terms are used and understood in the context of this book. From the discussion above, I would argue that the notion of equality in education as in (i) above is quite similar to the understanding of equal opportunity to access education as in (a); whereas equality in relation to educational outcomes (iii) relates closely to (b), equal educational opportunity for adult life as Coleman understands it. However, the notion of 'opportunity' acknowledges, I would argue, much more explicit the aspect

---

5 Summaries of these different approaches and their implications can, for example, be found in D'Olimpio, Gatley and Wareham (in press), Satz (2007) and Shields et al. (2023).

of choice and personal decision making to realise these opportunities rather than the expectation that everyone receives an identical outcome.

In this context, to complicate matters further, some have proposed the term *adequacy in education* (e.g., Satz, 2007). In short, adequacy in education proposes a defined standard of educational outcome for all (who are intellectually able) to reach as a minimum of state offered education. Any differences in educational outcomes and achievement beyond this standard are acceptable. As mentioned above, Satz (2007) proposes a brought understanding of citizenship (including aspects of job readiness, access to tertiary education, understanding and contributing to democratic processes, successful engagement with others, etc.) as this minimal outcome. Brighouse and Swift (2009), however, offer a critique that sees this minimum threshold as problematic as it allows for continuing significant inequalities in opportunities and access to higher positions and functions in society through additional support, beyond the adequacy threshold, of a selected student population, which are likely those who already have more opportunities and support through family and wealth. They argue that the notion of equality in education still requires consideration beyond the strive for adequacy as minimal standard for education outcomes. White (2011: 123–124) comments similarly, that some difference, some inequality is unavoidable and full equality potentially not even desirable, but that, with an eye on wellbeing and flourishing, inequalities in distribution of resources and possessions in society should not be allowed to be excessive.

The key challenge of the debate between equality and adequacy in education results from limited resources available to provide education for students. This said, we need to remind ourselves that education itself (i.e., knowledge, skills and understanding) is not a resource that is limited and can only be distributed to 'x' number of people. Education itself is limitless (in fact, its 'amount' grows with each person's learning and development); however, resources for teaching are not. Hence, the issue of equity and equality in education hinges on the distribution of resources (teacher time and support, learning tools, assistive technology, etc.) in the education system to support learning. The reason for this clarification being made here is that one could ask if an unequal distribution of educational resources to support learning can be considered 'just' if it entails that some students are not supported enough to reach their educational potential in an attempt to support other students so that all reach a similar level of 'adequate outcome' or 'adult opportunity'. This point brings us back to the opening paragraph considering the diversity of human beings. One challenge that is discussed in the literature in this regard is the so called 'bottomless pit problem' (Brighouse, 2003), which problematises a situation in which not enough resources in education might exist to ensure that all students, including all forms of differing abilities and diversity, can be supported sufficiently to reach a certain, externally defined, outcome level of adequacy or equal opportunity in life.

One line of argument for equal adult opportunity would be that an equal level of education, which supposedly leads to equal opportunities 'in occupation and otherwise' (Coleman, 1975: 28), contributes to a more equal society in terms of socio-economic outcomes; hence, reducing social inequality and leading to a more just society. This argument is similarly proposed by Satz (2007), envisioning their level of adequate education for citizenship to equalise society, which is countered by Brighouse and Swift (2009), pointing out that this approach still allows intellectual and economic elites to form, who would be able to occupy leading positions in society and economy, and which would perpetuate inequalities of access to power. The underlying idea, it seems to me, is that education alone is thought of as the instrument to solve inequality in society, which introduces a different aspect of the debate that hinges on varying readings of the term 'education' itself and is highly contested. It is the idea that education (in the meaning of qualification, which might or might not come with the intrinsic value of knowledge and understanding) provides positional opportunities in society through access to different levels of jobs and income. Another aspect, from a rights perspective, is the equal opportunity to participate in democratic processes, which arguably relates to positional opportunities; a third the notion of the equal right to experiencing the non-positional intrinsic goods of education (Brighouse, 2003; Shields et al., 2023). Each of these aspects, according to Shields et al., require a different approach or 'matrix' to equality in education. They are linked to educational aims and ends – what we see as the purpose(s) of education and schooling – and will be picked up again in the second part of this article. First, it is relevant to distinguish different meanings of the term 'education' itself, as they, I would argue, contribute to the challenges and some misunderstandings in the (at least public) debate of equality in education and equal educational opportunities.

Education, Schooling and Social Equity

The term *education* can be understood in different ways: (i) it can mean having knowledge, understanding, critical thinking skills, prudence, practical wisdom etc. – i.e., being educated; (ii) it can refer to the education system, most notably the schooling system – in the following referred to as 'schooling'; and (iii) it can point towards the education process – the interaction between teacher, student and subject matter[6]. The two relevant readings of education for the current topic are (i) and (ii), as I would suggest that proponents of the view that education can mitigate social inequality understand 'education' in the first meaning, presuming that schooling (as in ii) provides relevant educational outcomes. However, as Bowles and Gintis (2002) have argued, education systems are always embedded in a socio-cultural context and schooling has a tendency to not only reproduce but even to intensify socio-economic inequality. Although this effect seems to be mitigated by more integrated rather than selective education systems (cf. Liesen, 2005; Autio, 2021), it seems that schooling, due to its dependents on the external socio-cultural circumstances, is not a promising pathway to reduce existing socio-economic inequalities in a society.

However, does this mean that education, as understood in (i), is unsuitable to change social structure? I would argue not; although, it might not be sufficient in itself, and most certainly, it does not work the way current neoliberal, meritocratic positions assume: through the 'merit' of each individual (cf. Thrupp, 2007, 2008; Snook & O'Neill, 2010). I would argue that social change must be orchestrated structurally from a communal, governmental level, not from an individual level. Plenty of authors have argued and shown evidence that meritocracy is a myth, and family and social circumstances are much stronger predictors for economic success than a person's ability, education, and effort – or what is considered as personal 'merit' (e.g., Bowles & Gintis, 2002; Liesen, 2005; Thrupp, 2007, 2008; Snook & O'Neill, 2010). So how can education lead to social change?

I would suggest that education is able to support social change towards more social equality in two ways. First, if politicians are educated in a well-rounded, humanistic way that allows them to engage critically and in a reflected way with current meritocratic, neoliberal marketisation ideologies and their questionable application across large areas of social policy and society, education can play a role in the quality of policy decision making by government representatives who are regularly reflecting on their own beliefs, norms, values, and assumptions. Second, as democratic governments, at least in theory, are representatives of the people, a broad humanistic education for

---

[6] For a more detailed discussion of these different aspects of 'education', see Teschers (2018: 123–125).

all citizens would support the formation of governments that support such politics. Unfortunately, such broad education is under threat for some time, due to neoliberal, economy focused politics impacting on the education systems in many countries (cf. Roberts & Peters, 2008; Roberts & Codd, 2010). However, even if a broad humanistic education is endeavoured, education alone might not be enough, as indicated above. Andrew Peterson (2017), for example, argues that *compassion* needs to play a much stronger role in education and society to tackle social inequalities across all levels, small and large. I would argue that a combination of a broad humanistic education, which strengthens critical thinking and (self-)reflection, in combination with increased levels of compassion could go a long way to shift the cultural thinking and consciousness of a society. This should lead to a change in thinking and policy, away from punitive approaches and blaming individuals from a misled position of singular individual responsibility, towards a supportive social system that approaches inequality at a systemic level, acknowledging shared responsibility as a society. This is not to say that well educated, reflected and compassionate individuals do not already exist. However, it seems that so-called 'first world societies,' with the standard of wealth and living we find in many countries today, would have the resources to ensure that all people living in these countries are able to live in dignified circumstances: live in a healthy home; can afford healthy, regular meals; have access to all levels of (free) education; and have the opportunity to become valued members of their local communities, if these societies would choose to put the redistributing measures in place. Unfortunately, with the possible exception of some Scandinavian countries that seem to rank higher on the social equity scale, access to these, arguably basic, circumstances for a dignified life is lacking for many in most countries globally. Hence, compassionate self-reflected and critically thinking voices need to be strengthened further to promote a more just distribution of resources and opportunities in many modern countries and on a global scale, which *education*, as in understanding and knowledge, can support, but which schools, as institutions presumably offering an education, are not well positioned to provide alone without wider social change on national and global levels.

To summarise the key points made in this first part of the article, I have argued that much of the debate regarding equality and equity in education is complicated by sometimes not clearly defined terminology in some discourses, and a range of understandings for key terms, such as equality, equity, equal opportunity, fairness and justice in education, as well as what is meant by the term education itself. Different frames of reference for these terms further change the implications for practice in schools and other educational contexts. I have explained that 'education' can be understood in three different ways and a distinction is needed between education as *knowledge and understanding*, versus education as in *the education system*, i.e., schooling. Applying the expectation that society can be changed and become more equal through 'fixing' equality in schooling seems unreasonable; however, education as in knowledge, understanding and (practical) wisdom might play a role for society to become fairer and more just over time. I have further argued that, in the context of education, 'equality' understood as 'outcome equality' is quite similar in meaning to the currently public notion of 'equity' as in fairness and justice, implying the need for flexible (i.e., unequal) distribution of resources in schooling (teacher time, monetary support for assistive technology, flexible ways of representation/assessment, etc.) to reach somewhat *equal opportunities for adult life*. However, the focus on pre-defined, external educational outcomes for 'equal opportunities for adult life' (e.g., active citizenship) can leave us with the 'bottomless pit problem' as described by Brighouse (2003). In Part 2 of this article, I will propose a different understanding of what 'opportunities' might mean and entail in the context of an art of living, and argue that this broad understanding might also present a way to limit, and potentially overcome the bottomless pit problem in schooling.

Part 2: Exploring Equal Educational Opportunity and the Art of Living

Having explored some of the complexity of the debate around equality in education and equal educational opportunity, I aim to argue for a different perspective in the second part of this chapter, which might provide a partial solution to some of the issues indicated above. Following the summary above, after clarifying some of the conceptual understandings around equality in education, it seems that three key challenges remain for a focus on *equal educational opportunity*, understood as the *outcome* of schooling in form of formal education received, and the level of knowledge and skills accomplished, by students when they leave the formal education system. These challenges are: (a) what resembles a just distribution of educational resources for all students; (b) how to address the bottomless pit problem (Brighouse, 2003), when all available resources do not allow equal (or adequate) educational outcomes;

and (c) what 'opportunities' or 'outcomes' are referred to in a striving for equal educational (outcome) opportunities?

One could argue that equal access to education should be part of the list as well; however, I would argue that equal educational opportunities for all students requires fair and just access to education in the first place. Also, as mentioned above, education as knowledge/skills/understanding is not a finite resource in the sense that education of one person detracts from the pool of education/knowledge available for others. The means to teach and the support to learn and understand are limited, however, which is reflected in challenge (a). The aspects of access to education and distribution of resources becomes a particular problem through the diversity of students and people in general. This builds the foundation for the bottomless pit problem in challenge (b)[7]. The argument that I want to make here is that the issue of challenge (c) – what do we mean by opportunities or outcomes in education – is fundamental for the resolution, or not, of challenges (a) and (b). Hence, I will start with addressing challenge (c) first.

As indicated above, Coleman (1975) has discussed what is commonly understood by 'equal educational opportunity', drawing on rulings of the US Supreme Court:

> What appears to be at the base of the idea of equality of educational opportunity as used by the Court is a public educational system that is sufficiently effective to prevent, for normally intelligent children, the disadvantages that result from their family circumstances from handicapping them severely in adult life, in occupation and otherwise. (p. 28)

Coleman suggests the term 'equal educational adult opportunity' for more clarity. However, there are at least two issues with the implicit definition above: firstly, it is exclusive in nature, limiting the application of equal educational opportunity to 'normally intelligent children', hence excluding mental impairments that impact on the measurable intelligence of children; and, secondly, it seems to focus mainly on 'disadvantages that result from their family circumstances', which again potentially excludes other aspects of diversity of children (such as sex, gender identity, adverse life events, etc.). It further allows for a range of difference in outcome, implicitly allowing some 'handicapping' of students 'in occupation and otherwise' as long as these handicaps are not 'severe'. This is, one could argue, an acknowledgement that fully

---

7 Which proponents of the adequacy approach (Satz, 2007) tried to overcome, but according to Brighouse and Swift (2009) unsuccessfully so.

equal adult opportunities 'in occupation and otherwise' are not achievable through education for some reason or another. What is promising, although vaguely so, is the openness beyond occupational opportunities. Coleman, and the US Supreme Court, seem to acknowledge that the relevance of education for adult life reaches beyond occupation and economy, a view that is not always apparent considering the emphasis on STEM subjects, the obsession with measurability (Biesta, 2015), and policies affecting education through neoliberally driven functions of marketisation, managerialism and performativity (cf. Ball, 2016; Keddie, 2016).

Building on this aspect of 'otherwise', I argue that a potentially more promising approach to equality in education or 'equal educational opportunity' would be the equal opportunity for every student to develop their own art of living in an attempt to live a good and beautiful life, as discussed in earlier chapters. In summary, Schmid's art of living takes into account the uniqueness of each individual in their norms, values, beliefs, social and cultural background, interests, aspirations etc. Hence, Schmid prefers the notion of a 'beautiful life' to a 'good life' to emphasise that, just like a work of art, a life's beauty is a subjective notion and only the judgement of the person living this life is what actually counts, as other people's notion of what it means to live a good life might apply to them, but not to others. Such understanding would take into account the uniqueness of each individual and cater towards the diversity in society and humanity, as argued elsewhere:

> An art of living interpretation of equity would focus on an equal ability to develop one's own art of living and, hence, live a good and beautiful life despite the differences in living circumstances. For this, it is necessary to acknowledge the differences of individual human beings, cater for their individual development and learning processes, and to accept different educational outcomes and different foci on learning areas as an expression of individualism. In the end, every individual has a unique set of knowledge, experiences and skills, and a society should not try to 'normalise' its people but to offer opportunities for their diverse and unique abilities. (Teschers, 2013b: 186)

What is argued for here is a shift from an economic and occupational focus on education towards a more humanistic focus that considers each human being as a unique individual who can become the artist of their own life, shaping their own life and self, according to their wants, beliefs, norms and values under consideration of their individual circumstances (see also Teschers, 2013a, 2017, 2018). This approach likely includes an aspect of meaningful occupation and purposeful striving; however, it leaves the direction of this striving and occupation more directly in the hands of the student than any curriculum and prescribed external standards to be achieved. What this understanding of equity in education requires, however, is a society that is supportive of the diversity of every member, their interests, strengths, and aspirations. After all, technological advancement and economic growth have been a vehicle towards the improvement of the living circumstances and happiness of human beings. At some point in the last century, it seems, the vehicle has become the often-unquestioned purpose, as economic growth is seen, at least by advocates of neoliberal ideology, as the holy grail for human wellbeing. Csikszentmihalyi (2008: 1 & 10–16), however, points out that despite all economic growth and technical advancement, the happiness and life-satisfaction of people in developed countries has not increased over the last 50 somewhat years, rather on the opposite, and that the roots of this discontent are internal rather than external. Hence, it might be prudent as a society to ask the question: what, if not economic growth, increases people's happiness and life-satisfaction? After all, as Csikszentmihalyi also argues, 'no social system has ever survived long unless its people had some hope that their government would help them achieve happiness' (p. 77).

Some of the answers are explored by positive psychologists and include relationships, finding meaning in life through serving a purpose beyond one's own benefit, and increasing flow experiences, which can raise people's enduring happiness levels and life-satisfaction (cf. Seligman, 2010, 2011). As argued earlier (see Chapters Two & Three), these aspects resonate, and can be included, under the more holistic notion of engaging in an art of living approach towards shaping one's own life as a good and beautiful one. So, if we return to our challenge (c) above (what is meant by equal educational opportunities or outcomes), aiming schooling not solely towards gaining skills for job-readiness and potentially democratic citizenship (which arguably has not necessarily been a dominant focus of schooling for some time) but towards a more humanistic outcome of life-readiness that allows students to actively engage in shaping the direction of their own lives based on their interests, aspirations and personal circumstances (cf. Biesta, 2022), would allow for a wide variety of educational outcomes in terms of acquired knowledge and skills. However, equity could be achieved in terms of equal adult opportunities to strive towards a good and beautiful life and engage in an art of living, keeping in mind that ideas of what a good and beautiful life entails are individual, internal, and mitigated by unique personal circumstances. It also needs to be pointed out here that a beautiful life, as understood by Schmid (2000) and in this book, does not have to be a life of pure happiness and pleasures. As discussed earlier, even a life of hardship and challenges can be judged as a beautiful one by the person living this life as, for example, this person might value the personal character development and wisdom gained through overcoming life challenges. This is not to claim that creating or maintaining barriers for people is acceptable, but it is to acknowledge that life is complex, diverse, and unique for each individual and it is, at least in the near future, not possible to support everyone to do everything imaginable.

So, if we accept equal educational opportunities to engage in the art of living and to strive towards a good and beautiful life as a valid aim, if not to say an end of education, that, when achieved, constitutes equity and fairness in education, we can now consider what consequences result for the challenges (a) – fair distribution of resources, and (b) – the bottomless pit problem. First of all, focusing educational equity through schooling on the ability to develop an own art of living that can[8] lead towards a beautiful life, largely removes the requirement for external standards of educational achievement in terms of knowledge and academic skills for equity. Each person would have to be treated as unique individual and their learning journey and schooling experience adjusted to allow the development of necessary skills that allow an engagement in and development of their own an art of living. Beyond that, each person's aspirations, interests, wishes, norms, and beliefs would determine further learning, gathering of knowledge and acquisition of skills in the frame of each person's physical, mental and emotional abilities. This poses a range of new challenges however: (i) what skills and knowledge are necessary to be able to develop an own art of living? (ii) Does every person have the potential to achieve these skills and knowledge? (iii) At what point are children able to make their own judgement about their own learning journey and how much compulsory content/curriculum must be set by society and educators? There will certainly be further challenges from this shift in view, some of which are similar to existing challenges, others will be different. Overall, many challenges in education are subject to ongoing negotiations of each generation

---

8 Schmid (2000) acknowledges that there is no guarantee to that an individual who is able to develop their own art of living will end up with a life that they would consider a good and beautiful one due to circumstances outside of this person's control. However, such a person would at least actively strive towards such a life and have a more reasonable stab at a beautiful life than a person who let themselves be driven by external pressures rather than taking responsibility for their own decision making.

anew, as Dewey (1938) points out. The three points mentioned here seem most pertinent to me in the context of the matter at hand, however.

To address the first challenge (i), we can turn to Schmid (2000), who provides a list of knowledge areas that he sees as relevant to develop an own art of living in today's modern societies, on which I have expanded slightly in previous work with colleagues (Teschers, Neuhaus and Vogt, 2024). Schmid also indicates a range of skills which I would consider as more important than shifting areas of knowledge. This view resonates to some extent with Nussbaum and Sen's (1993) capability approach. The most notable faculty Schmid emphasises is the ability to see the interconnections [Zusammenhänge] in the world in order to take effective and targeted action. Some of the other skills Schmid indicates are the ability to reflect on one's own norms, values and beliefs – i.e., the ability to reflect and self-reflect. Schmid further identifies the development of prudence and practical wisdom, as in Aristotle's notion of *phronésis*, as essential for the art of living. Another aspect is *Bildung*, as in the process of self-formation and self-cultivation, which also supports the mentioned ability to understand the interconnections in the world. The German notion of *Bildung* is understood as a transformational process that goes beyond learning, to not just acquiring new knowledge but to be able to reflect on new knowledge and insights in a way so that it can affect one's self and character – shape the person one is and becomes. It includes, I would argue, the ability to learn, to think, to reflect and self-reflect, as well as a form of practical wisdom, as mentioned above. Schmid indicates in this context that *phronésis* can be learned through the process of *Bildung*. Following these considerations, we are left with a set of minimal requirements to have the potential to develop an own art of living: the ability to learn, to reflect on external matters (ideas, concepts, experiences), to self-reflect (norms, beliefs, values, etc.), the faculty of prudence and practical wisdom, and the ability to see the interconnections in the world for effective action[9], which provides direction for the second challenge (ii) above. The aforementioned aspect of prudence and practical wisdom, although important for many aspects of what Schmid considers essential in the context of the art of living, such as ethical considerations and an understanding of social conventions for living together in a society, is certainly desirable, but one could argue that a person not able to reach higher levels of practical wisdom can still engage in an art of living,

---

9 Although this can be minimised if a student struggles intellectually by making use of other people who have a better understanding of these matters – as such, seeing the connection between expressing a desire towards a caring person for possible change could be sufficient.

although with potentially less autonomy to ensure the safety of this person and people around them. The knowledge areas Schmid suggests as essential for the development of an own art of living, as will be discussed in Chapters Five and Six, can be summarised as cornerstones of a person's life cycle, such as birth, death, relationships, social structure, cultures, religion, challenges and meaning in life. The level of engagement with, and content of, each of these areas, however, would depend on each person's individual circumstances, as will be discussed in more detail in Chapter Six. As such, no set external level of 'knowledge' of these areas needs to be reached, but students should engage with these as much as is possible and relevant for them. Hence, the challenge (ii) of students' ability to learn and develop what is necessary for their own art of living is mitigated by their circumstances, and what they need is rather dependent on what they can achieve and are able to do in the first place.

Reflecting on the discussion above so far, it seems that equity in education as understood here (with the goal to enable each person to develop their own art of living towards living a good and beautiful life) is, on the one hand, more complex, as it is far more individualistic, and clear measurables can hardly be provided. On the other hand, provided we can arrange schooling to cater towards this goal, equity might be more readily achieved, and the bottomless pit problem (Challenge b) can be further minimised, if not overcome. This presumes, however, that society is organised in a way that allows every member to pursue what they consider a good and beautiful life to be, instead of following a semi-prescribed model of socially acceptable pathways, such as getting a degree, finding a job, finding a partner/family, settling down into some form of routine until retirement and eventually death. The constrictions of having to find a job that is relevant to current industry and economy is one of the major challenges in this context, I would argue. A basic income for all citizens might be a starting point to provide the kind of freedom that might not create the most economic productivity of a society, but potentially offer the more culturally productive – if we want to use this term in this context – opportunity. This can also increase social equality as people who are not able to engage in a productive form of work are not marginalised but provided with basic support regardless (without stigma), and who could be supported further on a needs' basis, as is already the case in many modern societies (more or less well).

To finalise the response to the challenge (a) above – fair distribution of resources – we can draw on the arguments of luck-egalitarianism (Calvert, 2014), who suggest that differences due to 'luck', may it be socio-economic differences or natural talents, should be mitigated, but not differences derived through active choices a person makes. I would argue that, in the context of an education for an art of living, this principle can be paired with the adequacy approach outlined above. According to Calvert, luck egalitarianists do not advocate to equalise everyone in education but recognise and cherish the inherent diversity of human beings. As such, the notion of an 'equal' outcome in terms of educational achievement can be seen as absurd. However, an equitable shot at living a 'good life', or a 'beautiful life' in our context, is not. Therefore, a fair distribution of resources in our context would mean that disadvantaged students, may it be social or natural disadvantage, should be specifically supported to the point at which the development of their own art of living and the pursuit of a beautiful life in their context is as feasible as it is for students with more advantaged backgrounds. The challenge, as mentioned before, is the complexity of human life and the challenge of measuring this feasibility. I would further suggest, slightly at odds with proponents of the adequacy model, that students who endeavour to engage in education beyond this minimal threshold should still be supported based on their needs, although there might be a shift in distribution of resources towards a more balanced distribution to allow all students to progress towards their respective potential.

While this leaves the final challenge (iii) – when are students able to make responsible decisions about their own learning and what content needs to be provided by schools and teachers in the interest of the wider society – unanswered here, I will return to this more pedagogical question in the following chapters.

Conclusion

As Calvert states, educational equality (or equity) is complex and pluralistic, with competing values at play. Therefore, there will likely never be a final and/or fixed answer to this conundrum. What I have argued in this chapter is a somewhat different measure or target for equity in education, or equal educational (outcome) opportunity, towards the ability of students to develop their own art of living and strive towards their own version of a beautiful life. I argued that equity in education needs to be focused on equal educational outcomes, which subsumes fair and just access to education as well as distribution of resources within education up to the point where the outcome threshold can be reasonably considered achieved. As such, a just and fair distribution of resources has to be un-equal to meet the diverse needs of students to develop the necessary abilities and understanding that enables them to develop their own art of living. Beyond this threshold, I would argue that a balance needs to be struck between the unequal distribution of resources to provide extra support for students who have higher developmental needs and the support provided to all students to develop their inherent talents and abilities. I see merit in both, the adequacy and the equity arguments made in the literature and, as such, I would argue that a balance needs to be negotiated between the two to continue to close the gap between luck of birth and the appropriate support to be provided to every student to develop their potential. While this does not quite fit what Rawls argued under the veil of ignorance, it seems prudent to me that such a setting would be desirable for people under the veil, not knowing where they enter into the education system. How such a system could then be designed and put into practice will be the focus of the following chapters.

References

Ainscow, M. (2012). Moving knowledge around: Strategies for fostering equity within educational systems. *Journal of Educational Change*, *13*(3), 289–310. doi:10.1007/s10833-012-9182-5.

Aristotle. (2002). *Nicomachean ethics*. Edited by J. Sachs. Newburyport, MA: Focus Publishing.

Autio, T. (2021). From Knowledge and Bildung Toward Competences and Skills in Finnish Curriculum Policy?: Some Theoretical, Historical, and Current Observations Related to Finland. *Euro-Asian Encounters on 21st-Century Competency-Based Curriculum Reforms: Cultural Views on Globalization and Localization*, 41–56. doi:10.1007/978-981-16-3009-5_3/COVER.

Ball, S. J. (2016). Subjectivity as a site of struggle: Refusing neoliberalism?. *British Journal of Sociology of Education*, *37*(8), 1129–1146. doi:10.1080/01425692.2015.1044072.

Ballard, K. (2012). Inclusion and social justice: Teachers as agents of change. In S. Carrington & J. MacArthur (Eds.), *Teaching in inclusive school communities* (pp. 65–87). Milton: John Wiley & Sons.

Bevan-Brown, J. (2006). Beyond policy and good intentions. *International Journal of Inclusive Education*, *10*(2–3), 221–234. doi:10.1080/13603110500392775.

Biesta, G. (2022). *World-centred education: A view for the present*. Routledge.

Biesta, G. J. J. (2015). *Good education in an age of measurement: Ethics, politics, democracy, good education in an age of measurement: Ethics, politics, democracy*. doi:10.4324/9781315634319.

Bowles, S., & Gintis, H. (1976). *Schooling in capitalist America*. London, England: Routledge & Kegan Paul.

Bowles, S., & Gintis, H. (2002). Schooling in capitalist America revisited. *Sociology of Education, 75*, 1–18.

Brighouse, H. (2003). Educational equality and justice. In *A companion to the philosophy of education*. Oxford, UK: Wiley, 471–486. doi:10.1002/9780470996454.ch34.

Brighouse, H. (2014). Equality, prioritising the disadvantaged, and the new educational landscape. *Oxford Review of Education, 40*(6), 782–798. doi:10.1080/03054985.2014.979013.

Brighouse, H., & Swift, A. (2009). Educational equality versus educational adequacy: A critique of Anderson and Satz. *Journal of Applied Philosophy, 26*(2), 117–128.

Calvert, J. (2014). Educational equality: Luck Egalitarian, pluralist and complex. *Journal of Philosophy of Education, 48*(1), 69–85. doi:10.1111/1467-9752.12048.

Coleman, J. S. (1975). What is meant by 'An Equal Educational Opportunity'. *Oxford Review of Education, 1*(1), 27–29.

Csikszentmihalyi, M. (2008). *Flow: The psychology of optimal experience*. [Modern classics ed.] New York, NY: Harper Perennial.

Dewey, J. (1938). *Experience and education*. New York, NY: Collier.

D'Olimpio, L., Gatley, J., & Wareham, R. (in press). *Philosophy of education*. Palgrave.

Gosepath, S. (2021). *Equality, Stanford Encyclopedia of Philosophy*. Available at: https://plato.stanford.edu/entries/equality/ (Accessed: 12 May 2023).

Institute for Policy Studies. (2023). *Income Inequality – Inequality.org*. Available at: https://inequality.org/facts/income-inequality/ (Accessed: 12 May 2023).

Keddie, A. (2016). Children of the market: Performativity, neoliberal responsibilisation and the construction of student identities. *Oxford Review of Education, 42*(1), 108–122. doi:10.1080/03054985.2016.1142865.

Liesen, C. (2005). Equality of opportunity as a rationale for inclusive education. In *International special education conference*. Glasgow, Scotland.

Miller, D. (2017). Justice. *Stanford Encyclopedia of Philosophy* [Preprint]. Available at: https://plato.stanford.edu/archives/fall2017/entries/justice/ (Accessed: 12 May 2023).

Nussbaum, M. C., & Sen, A. K. (1993). *The quality of life*. Oxford, UK: Oxford University Press.

Peters, R. S. (1966). *Ethics and education*. London, England: George Allen & Unwin.

Peterson, A. (2017). *Compassion and education*. Palgrave Macmillan.

Rawls, J. (2001). *Justice as fairness: {A} restatement*. Edited by E. Kelly. Cambridge, MA: Harvard University Press.

Roberts, P., & Codd, J. (2010). Neoliberal tertiary education policy. In M. Thrupp & R. Irwin (Eds.), *Another decade of {N}ew {Z}ealand education policy: {W}here to now?* Hamilton, New Zealand: Wilf Malcolm Institute of Educational research, 99–110.

Roberts, P., & Peters, M. A. (2008). *Neoliberalism, higher education and research*. Rotterdam, Netherlands: Sense Publishers.

Satz, D. (2007). Equality, adequacy, and education for citizenship. *Ethics, 117*(4), 623–648. doi:10.1086/518805.

Schmid, W. (2000). *Schönes Leben?: Eine Einführung in die Lebenskunst*. Frankfurt, Germany: Suhrkamp.

Seligman, M. E. P. (2010). *Authentic happiness: Using the new positive psychology to realise your potential for lasting fulfillment*. London, England: Nicholas Brealey Publishing.

Seligman, M. E. P. (2011). *Flourish: A visionary new understanding of happiness and well-being.* New York, NY: Free Press.

Shields, L., Newman, A., & Satz, D. (2023). *Equality of Educational Opportunity*, Stanford Encyclopedia of Philosophy. Available at: https://plato.stanford.edu/entries/equal-ed-opportunity/ (Accessed: 4 May 2023).

Snook, I., & O'Neill, J. (2010). Social class and educational achievement: {B}eyond ideology. *New Zealand Journal of Educational Studies*, 45(2), 3–18.

Teschers, C. (2013a). An educational approach to the art of living. *Knowledge Cultures*, 1(2), 25–32.

Teschers, C. (2013b). *Education and the art of living.* University of Canterbury. doi:10.26021/9795.

Teschers, C. (2017). A BEAUTIFUL LIFE AS AN END OF EDUCATION. *Knowledge Cultures*, 5(6), 62–73. doi:10.22381/KC5620175.

Teschers, C. (2018). *Education and Schmid's art of living, Education and Schmid's art of living.* Routledge. doi:10.4324/9781315563848.

Teschers, C., Neuhaus, T., & Vogt, M. (2024). Troubling the boundaries of traditional schooling for a rapidly changing future – Looking back and looking forward. *Educational Philosophy and Theory*, (early online), 1–12. doi:10.1080/00131857.2024.2321932.

Thrupp, M. (2007). Educations's `inconvenient truth': Part one – Persistent middle class advantage. *New Zealand Journal of Teachers' Work*, 4(2), 77–88.

Thrupp, M. (2008). Education's 'inconvenient truth': Part two – The middle classes have too many friends in education. *New Zealand Journal of Teachers' Work*, 5(1), 54–62.

Uhl, S. (2001). Die Aufgaben derAllgemeinen Pädagogik: Eine Klassifikation der gängigen Auffassungen. [The Tasks of a General Theory of Education: A classification of current thoughts]. *Zeitschrift für Erziehungswissenschaft*, 4, 61–82.

White, J. (2011). *Exploring well-being in schools : A guide to making children's lives more fulfilling.* Routledge.

· 5 ·

THE ART OF LIVING AS AN END OF EDUCATION

While I have argued in earlier work (Teschers, 2017) for the relevance of the Art of Living as overarching aim, or end, of education, it is necessary here to summarise the earlier argument and outline some of the contentions and complexities surrounding the notion of aims and ends in education. I will then expand on the earlier arguments made and discuss how my proposed art of living approach to education resonates with other related positions, such as Biesta's (2022) *World-Centred Education* and the argument that *flourishing* should be the overarching end of education.

Exploring Aims and Ends in Education

In previous work (Teschers, 2013, 2017, 2018), I have argued that the development of students' own art of living ought to be one of the aims, if not *the end* of education – the main purpose of the educational endeavour. For my earlier argument, I have strongly relied on examining the position of two significant educational theorists: John Dewey and R. S. Peters. While I will start with an abbreviated summary of the past argument here, the focus of this chapter will lie on positioning and linking my argument for an education for the art of living and a beautiful life to other contemporary theorists. My aim is to show that what I am calling for in my work is not outlandish or singular, but relatable and complimentary to other current thinkers who have considered what education and schooling *should* be for and aiming at. I have two main reasons for this endeavour: for one, my work linking the art of living (and particularly Schmid's approach) with educational theory and practice is still somewhat unique[1], and, therefore, I see the need to show its compatibility with, and differences to, other related strands of thinking; and, second, I believe that this approach has something to offer that can fundamentally change how we see and approach education, and schooling (I will explain this distinction below), with potentially significant positive implications for our social cohesion and our quality of life, as alerted to in earlier chapters.

Before I start with the quick review of my earlier argument, it is necessary to clarify some of the terminology I am using that is of particular relevance for arguments about aims in and ends of education. First of all, it seems prudent to clarify what I mean by 'education'. I find the term 'education' in the English language problematic as it subsumes a number of different concepts that are related but also somewhat different. In German, Eckard Liebau (1999) offers three concepts that make up the German understanding of *Pädagogik* [Education]: *Erziehung* [upbringing; raising; includes socialisation], *Bildung* [(self-) formation and cultivation], and *Entfaltung* [flourishing]. Gert Biesta (2022) picks up on the earlier two and argues the distinction between three spheres or 'purposes' of education: *subjectification, socialisation,* and *qualification* (I will expand on these below). And I have explained before (Teschers, 2017) that I see at least three different ways in which 'education' as a term is used in the English language. These include (i) education as the process of teaching and learning[2]; (ii) education as something akin to *Bildung* (i.e., having an understanding of the world and oneself, which is sometimes reflected in the phrase 'having an education'); and (iii) education referring to the (compulsory) education system which could be termed 'schooling'. These three are obviously related as what is going on in schools and the education system (iii) is (ideally, although debatable[3]) the process of education (i), which then (again ideally) might lead to the students being educated, i.e., having *Bildung*

---

1   I want to note that many colleagues have shown interest in this work and I have collaborated with others, such as Maria Nieto (Colombia), Laura D'Olimpio (UK), Michaela Vogt (Germany), Till Neuhaus (Germany) and Te Hurinui Clarke (New Zealand), progressing this agenda.

2   Biesta (2022) refers to this by stating his use of education to be as a verb, the 'doing' of education or the relational practice between a student and an educator engaging with a theme/object of study.

3   See, for example, Biesta (2015, 2022) for a critique of what is happening in schools, which sometimes is more alike to 'training' (the acquisition of skills and knowledge without regard

(ii) and a working understanding of the world in which to act with purpose and guided by ethical and moral standards[4]. It needs to be said, though, that education is not limited to schools and centres (e.g., early childhood education). As Liebau (1999) contests, education in its broader sense (understood beyond the limitations of academic learning[5]), including *Erziehung, Bildung,* and *Entfaltung,* is a life-long process of personal self-formation, cultivation and becoming. It can happen everywhere and anytime through, for example, experiences and engagement with the world, relations and engagement with others, and/or contemplation. As such, I use education as a holistic and broad term that includes all aspects that contribute to the development of a human being inside and outside of schools and the education system. So, when I argue for the art of living as an *end of education*, I refer to this broader understanding of the term. However, this is not to say that this will not have implications for schools and centres. On the contrary, schools and centres as part of national education systems, especially in form of compulsory education, have a significant role and responsibility (due to their time-consuming compulsory nature) to support this overarching end of education. Like other positions I will discuss below, I would argue that schooling that focuses on a narrow understanding of 'education,' more akin to 'training' of academic skills and knowledge alone, falls short of what Biesta (2013, 2015, 2022), for example, calls 'good education': a balanced approach to subjectification, socialisation, and qualification (instead of a singular focus on qualification).

So, after having clarified my broader understanding of education as a project of human development - or becoming one could say - and having clarified the relationship between education and schooling as a subset of the wider educational endeavour, I will now briefly turn to the distinction between *aims* and *ends* of education, drawing on my earlier argument utilising Dewey's (1916/2008) and R. S. Peters' (1973) writing on the matter. For my understanding of the distinction between aims and ends, I found Dewey's writing particularly helpful. Dewey states that a proper *end of education* would be 'the promotion of the best possible realization of humanity as humanity' (2008: 100). In

---

of the subjectivity of the students) than 'education' (the becoming of a self and the holistic development of a human being to find their place in and relationship with the world).

4 For a more detailed discussion of the underlying ethics of Schmid's art of living see Teschers (2018). Biesta (2022) also explains the importance of 'being in the world without being the centre of the world' which relates to Schmid's ethical position, which I will touch on later.

5 See Biesta's (2015, 2022) critique of the discourse of 'learnification' and its reduction of what education is and should be.

comparison, he states that *aims in education* are manifold and need to be negotiated by every generation anew. Here he states three main categories that seem to encapsulate most of people's aims in education: the natural development of the individual (cf. Rousseau); 'social efficiency' and socialisation; and personal mental enrichment or 'culture' (2008: 129). Without wanting to dive deeper into Dewey's categorisation of aims, it becomes clear in his writing that aims can be understood as temporary (every generation needs to renegotiate them), local contextual (culturally and nationally), and can vary dependent on who is formulating these aims (e.g., students' aims might be different from teachers' aims, or politicians' aims, or parents' aims and expectations, etc.). Aims are often formulated as something to be achieved, measurable, and somewhat limited in focus, such as 'to be able to read and write' and similar. On the other hand, Dewey understands an 'end of education' as an overarching concept that is enduring, holistic, broad in scope, and somewhat intrinsic to the idea of education. R. S. Peters (1973), on the other hand, contends that education should not be subjugated to any overarching aim or end, as, he argues, all external aims on education will make education a means to an end. He claims that even well intended ends, such as the best life for most people, would bear the danger of being instrumentalised, and indeed, he states, terrible things have been done by passionate (and fanatic) advocates of final ends of education (1973: 130–131). Instead, Peters argues for education to be an end in itself, as 'there is a quality of life embedded in the activities which constitute education, and ... "life" must be for the sake of education, not education for life' (1973: 131). However, I have argued before (Teschers, 2017, 2018) that I see a distinction here between extrinsic aims that are attributed to education and then proclaimed as a final end, and, what I call, intrinsic ends that are essential to the idea of education, which is *to enable people to engage in and develop their own art of living in support of the pursuit of their own beautiful life*[6]. To close the loop with Dewey's notion of 'the best possible realization of humanity as humanity' as proper end of education, I draw on German *Bildung*-Idealism, which, according to Liebau (1999), claims that such 'perfection' of humanity can only be achieved through the development of the human potential of each person, which requires *Bildung* and the engagement with education as a life-project, as called for by Peters. The 'quality of

---

6 I use this formulation as living a beautiful life is not a given, according to Schmid, even when one is engaged in the art of living. All we can do is to strive towards such ends but not all is in our control and so we might fail. The important part is that we actively try rather than let ourselves be driven by external forces alone.

life' that comes through the engagement with education, as Peters claims, I argue, is related to the notion of a *beautiful life* and the development of one's own art of living, and, therefore, an intrinsic end of education. Still, we need to heed Peters' caution that stating this end, if misunderstood, can lead to improper application in practice.

The Art of Living and Biesta's World-centred Education

Having summarised my argument for the development of students' own art of living as an end of education to date, I will now draw links between Gert Biesta's work regarding the functions and purpose(s) of education in relation to my argument and Schmid's approach to the art of living. I have selected Biesta's work here for various reasons. First, because Biesta has developed a careful critique of the language used in the discourse about (and in) education and schooling that shines a light on, and gives words[7] to, the challenging developments in education in recent history (at least over the last 20–30 years, but arguably even before that; cf. Teschers, Neuhaus & Vogt, 2024). However, Biesta's work not only highlights the challenges, of which there are many, but also proposes a way forward by clarifying the purpose of education and argues what education should ultimately be for, which is topical for the discussion in this chapter. I aim to show here that much of Biesta's argument regarding the functions and purpose of education resonates with Schmid's art of living and my argument that education ought to aim towards the development of people's own art of living. In doing so, I do not claim to present an exhaustive comparison of the two concepts. Considering the richness and level of detail of both accounts, this would warrant a book of its own. However, I intend to highlight the links between both approaches for education to show that they are relatable on many levels, while remaining distinct in focus and aspiration. In fact, I would argue that both approaches are complimentary and can refine our understanding of education itself and the role it (and schooling) can play for the 'best possible realisation of humanity', to use Dewey's phrase again.

---

7   Biesta coined, for example, the term 'learnification'; alerted to the 'age of measurement' in education; expressed the functions of education as 'subjectification', 'socialisation, and 'qualification'; encouraged educators to take the 'beautiful risk' in education; and argued for a move towards a 'world-centred' education.

To start, I will draw on the three functions of education Biesta (2022)[8] identifies for 'good education': *subjectification, socialisation,* and *qualification*. I will elaborate on the latter two below and start with 'subjectification', as this is likely the most difficult to understand[9] but also the most fundamental in relation to Schmid's art of living. Subjectification, in Biesta's reading, is concerned with the *becoming of the 'I'* – the becoming of *a* self, an active agent in the world (p. 33). It is listed first here, as Biesta sees it as the basis for education and the foundation for schooling (p. 8). Without a formative subject[10], the best we can hope to achieve in school settings is training, not education. Training, Biesta argues, does not require a thinking and active self, it only requires absorption and regurgitation of information or processes. Training treats students as objects that need to 'learn' what is presented, which can be measured through the achievement of 'learning outcomes' (p. 50)[11]. Education, on the other hand, is more than learning; it supports students to become a thinking, acting self that exists in relationship with the world (pp. 60–61). He describes subjectification as the 'existential paradigm' of education (in contrast to the 'cultivation paradigm' currently dominating schooling and education systems) as it focuses on providing the student (as subject) with the opportunity to be in relation with the world and develop the knowledge and skills to navigate the world (p. 8). To illustrate this, Biesta presents the 'Parks-Eichmann Paradox' (pp. 25–40): he explains how Rosa Parks shows her 'I', her 'being there' as an active agent in the world by not following the discriminatory rule of where to sit and not to sit on the bus as a person of colour; whereas Eichmann, a German Nazi officer, argued during the Nürnberg trials that he was not to blame for his actions as he was just following orders – i.e., he was 'not there' as an active agent and just a passive

---

8   Biesta has developed his arguments over some time across multiple publications. While I will refer to some of these where appropriate, much has led to a culmination in his latest book *World-centred Education: A view for the present* (2022) and my argument here is largely based on this latest work if not otherwise indicated.

9   I can only provide a very abbreviated account of the concept here; for the interested reader, Biesta dedicates Chapter 4 in his latest book *World-centred Education* to this topic.

10 Biesta chooses the term 'subject' here not in the meaning of being subjected to or by someone, but in the continental/German reading of a being with subjectivity in contrast to being an object of manipulation or educational intervention.

11 Unfortunately, this form of training rather than education has become more common in school settings due to the changing discourse of 'learnification' and neoliberal ideological influences of performativity and measurement in policy and curriculum that influence teachers' work and practice (cf. Biesta, 2022: 60–63; O'Neill, 2023).

follower. Eichmann took his 'I', his 'self' out of the equation, Biesta argues. Subjectification then is exactly about supporting students not to become passive pawns following other people's directive but to be active, thinking agents that make their own decisions based on their own moral compass. And this is where the first link between Biesta's subjectification and Schmid's art of living emerges. For Schmid, the art of living is about taking responsibility for one's own life and actively shaping one's own life rather than being driven by external forces and expectations. Biesta's 'becoming of a self' and being able to make decisions when called upon by the world, I argue, is exactly what Schmid means when he is calling for the person engaged in the art of living to take responsibility for their own life, their own actions, and to make their own decisions based on their own norms, values and beliefs, i.e., their own moral compass. Subjectification, the existential question of being and becoming an active agent in the world, is the foundation for both Biesta's notion of world-centred education and Schmid's art of living.

Biesta then argues that as an active agent, as a subject, one needs to develop a relationship to one's own desires and a relationship with the world (2022: 10). One needs to understand what is desirable not just for oneself but also from a view of the Other and the world. As such, his title of *world-centred education* emphasises this relationship of being 'in the world but not at the centre of the world'. This ethical relationship between one's self and the world is mirrored in Schmid's ethics of the art of living, which he bases on the Aristotelean notion of *phronésis*, as discussed earlier in Chapter Three. Schmid, similar to Biesta, argues that as individuals engaged in the art of living, we need to understand that we are in relationship with others and the world and moderate our behaviour, our gestures [German: Gesten] as Schmid calls them, towards desirable actions. For Schmid, this reflection on one's actions is moderated by the view towards an environment that is supportive of the developments of every person's own art of living and their pursuit of a beautiful life. As such, it requires dialogue, negotiation, and compromise between one's own desires and what is desirable from a world-centred perspective.

Circling back to the development of an art of living as the end of education, as I argue for here, Biesta's first function of education, subjectification, is a fundamental aspect of working towards this end. To be able to take responsibility for our own life and shape it actively, we need to develop agency and a sense of self that does not shy away from making uncomfortable decisions when called upon 'by the world' – by the circumstances we find ourselves in. This requires a form of 'existential education' (2022: 36): the teasing out and support of the development of the 'I' of the student, which brings us back to the notion of *Bildung*. Biesta's reading of *Bildung* as self-formation of the 'I' and transformation of one's self is also central to Schmid's art of living. It is a life-long process of becoming, or a 'care of the self'[12], that ought to be supported in schools and centres. For Biesta, this existential work of education of the development of *a self* for students and enabling them to form a relationship with the world is a key purpose of education, which is further supported by, and also a prerequisite for, the two other purposes of socialisation and qualification.

Socialisation and qualification, in contrast to subjectification, arguably fall under the cultivation paradigm of education. Biesta (2013: 128) defines *qualification* as 'ways in which education qualifies people for doing things – in the broad sense of the word – by equipping them with knowledge, skills, and dispositions.' This is currently the main dimension of schooling, he contends, and while it is an important aspect of schooling, it should not be the only one – or the dominant one, considering the argument above. The third purpose of education for Biesta is *socialisation*, which 'has to do with the ways in which, through education, we become part of existing social, cultural and political practices and traditions' (ibid.). In short, it is about introducing 'newcomers', which for Biesta can be children or those coming from other countries, into existing social, cultural and political orders. Biesta generally argues for a balanced approach of schooling towards these three purposes of education.

For Schmid's art of living, socialisation and qualification play a significant role to enable students to act effectively in the world. Schmid argues that to be able to act effectively, one needs to be able to see the 'interconnections' [German: Zusammenhänge] in the world – to understand the workings of the world, one could say. This requires an understanding of the social, cultural and political norms, values, and institutions, as well as a general understanding of the subject matters concerning the workings of the world. It is also somewhat self-evident that to be able to shape one's life actively, one needs to be able to survive in the world, which, in today's societies, means that one needs to be able to pursue some form of work that provides the means for survival and the pursuit of whatever one considers a beautiful life to be. Hence, qualification (the ability to do things) and socialisation (navigating social structures) are important domains of both Biesta's approach to education and Schmid's art of living. However, as the domain of qualification is already well

---

12 Schmid (2000a) draws on Foucault's (1984) work of *The Care of the Self* in this context.

implemented in education systems today, Schmid suggests a range of themes that seem important to the socialisation dimension and to understanding the social, cultural and political world in which we find ourselves in. These themes are: '*the human being as individual; the social human being; difficulties and burdens of human life; striving for fulfilment and meaning in life; religions, beliefs and cultures of humanity; and the personal shape of one's life and global perspectives*' (Teschers, 2017: 69–70; italics in original). In work undertaken with colleagues, we argue for three further themes that, while potentially overlapping in some respect with these proposed by Schmid, add aspects that we consider relevant for today's context: '*economic structures of human societies; legal, political and governmental organisation of human co-existence; and potentially science, technology and the arts of humanity*' (Teschers et al., 2024). While the latter theme starts to bridge into the domain of qualification with the aspects of science and technology, we added this theme here as a more rounded consideration of what is important for the development of an art of living, as well as to emphasise that *the arts* play an equally important role to the other two domains, which seems to be more and more forgotten in schooling curricula, policy and the education discourse.

To summarise, I have shown above that Biesta's concept of *world-centred education* and Schmid's art of living as an overarching end of education are not just compatible but complimentary. Biesta's notion of subjectification as a key purpose of education is fundamental for Schmid's art of living and as such is an important aspect of educational practice in schools and centres to support the development of students' own art of living. Schmid, on the other hand, provides some guiding themes for further curriculum development to strengthen the dimension of socialisation with a view on understanding the interconnections in the world to allow the subject to act purposefully and effectively in their endeavour to shape their own lives actively. I will expand on these aspects in more detail in the following chapter. However, first it seems relevant to address the recent calls for *flourishing* as a possible aim or end of education.

Flourishing and an Education for the Art of Living

Calls for *human flourishing* as an aim or even the end of education have grown over the last two decades (e.g., de Ruyter, 2004; Brighouse, 2008; White, 2011; Kristjánsson, 2019; D'Olimpio, Gatley & Wareham, 2024). These calls coincide with an increased attention on wellbeing and the re-emergence of Aristotle's virtues ethics, including his notion of *eudaimonia*, in philosophy since the 1980s, going back to MacIntyre's (1981) *After Virtue*. Flourishing, inspired by Aristotle's work, has also seen increased attention in neighbouring disciplines such as positive psychology. Kristjánsson (2012, 2019: 29), for example, discusses how positive psychologists claim links between their concepts and understanding of flourishing and liken them to Aristotle's *eudaimonia*. However, Kristjánsson also points out that the interpretation used by advocates of the concept of flourishing in positive psychology is somewhat removed from Aristotle's original concept and also from more recent, and to some extend more flexible, neo-Aristotelian understandings. Nevertheless, positive psychology has made inroads into education as a discipline through the wellbeing debate in education and Seligman's call for 'positive education' (a somewhat unhelpful term in my view[13]), proposing a psychological take on 'flourishing' as a key aim, if not end of education. However, Kristjánsson (2012) explains that much of what positive psychology tries to push onto education in form of 'positive education' is nothing new but has long been part of the education tradition in theory and practice. This is not to say that (positive) psychology has nothing to offer education. I do think that in education, we can learn and make use of much what psychologists uncover. As such, psychology has its place, but in my mind, it is one bridge too far to constitute a psychological interpretation of 'flourishing' (or 'wellbeing' for that matter) as the guiding norm for educational practice. While this idea of a measurable and tightly defined form of flourishing with somewhat clear predictors and causalities is certainly appealing to proponents of neoliberal ideology in politics and policy, it can quickly fall into the measurement trap alerted to by Biesta (2015), asking the question if we 'measure what we value, or rather value what we (can) measure'?

Therefore, Kristjánsson, and others mentioned above, draw on Aristotle's philosophical tradition – not(!) positive psychology definitions – to call for

---

13 The term 'positive education' seems derived from Seligman's original push for 'positive psychology' as a reversal of the focus of psychology from the negative (what is wrong with people) to the positive (what supports people's wellbeing). While positive education tries to show the link to positive psychology, it seems to imply that education before 'positive education' was not 'positive' but something else (e.g., focused on the 'negative'). This connotation of the term does not make sense in my understanding of education as an endeavour that always aimed towards human development in some form (i.e., towards the betterment of the human condition).

flourishing (understood as a translation of Aristotle's *eudaimonia*) as an end of education. While I find the term 'flourishing' problematic as a translation of *eudaimonia*[14], among others due to the differing understanding of what 'flourishing' means and entails in different contexts (i.e., psychology, philosophy, education) and the current dominance of psychological and medical discourses in the wellbeing debate at large and in education in particular, I will adopt Kristjánsson's (2019) definition of flourishing to discuss its relation to Schmid's art of living and explain why I see the latter as a more appropriate end of education. I intend to show that, while human flourishing is a desirable vision or driver for most (if not all) human undertaking, and it is related to Schmid's art of living and a beautiful life, Schmid's concept seems to me somewhat closer to the process involved to reach *eudaimonia*, in Aristotle's terms, and what reasonably can be achieved in and through education.

As *flourishing* is, however, also not unanimously defined in philosophy, I use Kristjánsson's (2019: 1) definition here as it seems to me the most developed (although not the most accessible), I have come across, and Kristjánsson's account of flourishing as an end of education the most convincing[15]:

> *Human flourishing* is the (relatively) unencumbered, freely chosen and developmentally progressive activity of a meaningful (subjectively purposeful and objectively valuable) life that actualises satisfactorily an individual human being's natural capacities in areas of species-specific existential tasks at which human beings (as rational, social, moral and emotional agents) can most successfully excel.

This definition is somewhat challenging in so far as it captures a range of aspects of the concept and refines the understanding of the terminology to achieve a form of clarity of meaning. I will unpack this meaning further, while comparing parts with Schmid's concept of the *art of living*, which can be defined as 'the wholehearted attempt, due to [... one's responsibility for one's own life], to take ownership of one's life in a timely manner, and to potentially shape it into a "beautiful life"' (Schmid, 2000b: 7, my translation). As this definition is also not the most accessible, I list the key parts again in other

---

14 Flourishing, however, is a much better translation for *eudaimonia* than 'happiness', which has been used historically and, as de Ruyter (2004: 337–338) states, "has hedonistic overtones and often a too narrow focus on particular feelings and states of a person."

15 Kristjánsson himself is an esteemed scholar and deeply familiar with Aristotelian thought. Hence, I defer to his expertise here in how 'human flourishing' that is based on a neo-Aristotelian understanding of *eudaimonia* can reasonably be defined to discuss its relevance for education.

words, which include that one actively cares for the direction one's life is taking – rather than be driven by external expectations, one has to take action to shape one's life instead – and while one might strive towards one's own version of a 'beautiful life' (judgement of which lies in the eyes of the person living said life), one might not be successful even though one is engaged in the process of the art of living.

Bringing both concepts together, it is noteworthy that, as a first parallel, both Schmid and Kristjánsson seem to take a neo-Aristotelian approach in their understanding of *eudaimonia*: both emphasise the subjective aspects of human flourishing and seem to believe that *eudaimonia* is something that can be achieved by many, not just a rare few. As such, neither the art of living nor flourishing should be considered an 'elitist' ideal but as an achievable endeavour – which is relevant and reassuring from an educational perspective. A second parallel is the importance that both place on *phronésis* as a mediating faculty that allows individuals to moderate their behaviour towards a virtuous life (Kristjánsson) or the development of an 'enlightened self-interest' (Schmid) that requires a person to consider others and one's environment in their decision-making. Drawing on Kristjánsson's definition above, both concepts rely on a certain level of freedom for decision making without which an active shaping of one's own life would not be possible (which could then lead to a flourishing life). Meaning in life is also present in both approaches and Schmid (2000a: 294), similarly, refers to the subjective perspective as well as objective value of one's take of meaning in life. Kristjánsson's notion of 'satisfactory actualisation' of one's capacities relates to Schmid's active shaping of one's own life along one's personal norms, values, and beliefs, and within the constraints of one's natural abilities and external circumstances.

Arguably, flourishing, as defined by Kristjánsson, requires a higher level of freedom, whereas Schmid's art of living would allow to 'find' meaning and live a life that the person living it can judge as 'beautiful', even if constraints existed that would prevent it from being considered a 'flourishing' life. To illustrate this point, we can draw on the Stephen Hawking's example Kristjánsson (2019: 22–23) discusses. Kristjánsson explains that, while Hawking has certainly lived a life with many successes and huge achievements – personally and for humankind – he has not lived a life that one could call a 'flourishing' life due to his significant health impediments (which Hawking confirmed himself, according to Kristjánsson). From an art of living perspective, it is at least not impossible that Hawking could have consider his life a 'beautiful' one regardless of the health issues he faced. The notion of a 'beautiful life' does not exclude hardship but is rather pointed towards how a person sees their own life (in retrospect) as a whole and if they would say that it was a life worthwhile living; a life that, while not perfect, has been a life one can stand by and be contend with based on one's own norms, values, beliefs and aspirations. While ideally it would be a life with abandon of objective beauty, pleasure, and happiness, this is not a necessity for it to be judged as 'beautiful' by the person having lived their life. Another example (in fact many) can be found in the glamourous lives of celebrities past and present. While on the surface many have a life of abundance (physical health, money, luxury, and beautiful things), not few have faced significant experiences of despair and emotional suffering, and it is questionable if all would (have) consider their life a 'beautiful one' when reflecting back on personal norms, values, and beliefs and how they lived their life in relation to these. Of course, it needs to be pointed out now that such experiences of despair and suffering would again preclude these people from being considered 'flourishing' in that moment and, provided they overcome this episode and move on from there, would still allow them to judge their life as beautiful – maybe precisely due to the experiences of hardship and suffering that allowed them to grow and become 'better' human beings based on their subjective norms and values.

What follows from this contemplation is a key distinction between the flourishing idea and Schmid's concept of the art of living, which is that the first is a state to be achieved, such as the state of *eudaimonia*; the latter, however, is a way of living, a process and practice of approaching life in an artful and maybe artistic manner that might lead to a 'beautiful life' but also might fail. As such, the key difference I see between the two is in their nature, their essence if you will: the one is a state of being, the other a way of life. And while both strongly draw on notions of Aristotle's work, again *flourishing* seems to be aimed towards the 'end product' one could say, whereas the *art of living* emphasises the procedural aspects of Aristotle's philosophy. Now, one could argue that proponents of flourishing as an end of education do include the procedural aspects in their argument and that these are precisely what educators need to focus on to enable their students to flourish[16]. This then highlights one challenge for proclaiming flourishing as the end of education: for students

---

16 Here it needs to be pointed out that there is a difference between flourishing *in* education and flourishing *through* education. The first is arguably more the focus of positive psychology and the positive education movement; whereas the latter is more the focus of Kristjánsson's, and others work, calling for flourishing as an end of education.

to flourish, several pre-conditions need to be met that lie outside of the sphere of teachers and educators[17].

As the two main pre-conditions for flourishing, Kristjánsson names '*external necessities . . . and a sense of meaning and purpose*' (p. 33; italics in original). For the first, Kristjánsson (p. 35) lists six categories, based on Aristotle, with the one or other small amendment from the original theory: (1) close parental attachment and good upbringing/education; (2) good government, ruling in the interest of the people, and a just constitution; (3) enough wealth to make sure we do not 'come a cropper'; (4) a complete life: namely, a life in which we do not die prematurely; (5) health, strength and even minimal physical beauty; and (6) friends and family to help hone one's virtues, and making a contribution to the continuation of our species[18]. While all these suggested necessities for flourishing can play a role in the art of living and might contribute to one's concept of a beautiful life, I contend that none of these are necessary to engage in the art of living – although an absence of all of these would make the development of one's own art of living and pursuit of a beautiful life challenging.

The second pre-condition, to have a sense of meaning and purpose, Kristjánsson explains to be necessary but not sufficient for flourishing. As such, he contests the notion taken by some theorists that flourishing can be seen as synonymous with a quest for purpose or meaning in life. However, he cautions that a sense of 'meaning' or 'purpose' in life is subjective and can potentially be 'amoral or even immoral' (p. 41). He draws on Hitler as example of someone who certainly had an internal purpose that gave him meaning, which is qualitatively widely different from the purpose or meaning that is derived from 'doing moral deeds [, which] lends most purpose to people's lives' (p. 41). In regard to Schmid's art of living, 'meaning' and 'purpose' are discussed slightly differently: Schmid (2000a) distinguishes between *Sinn des Lebens* [meaning of life] (p. 169), which arguably sits akin to Kristjánsson's take of having a sense of meaning in life; and *Sinn im Leben finden* [making sense of life] and *dem Leben Sinn geben* [to give meaning to one's life] (p. 294). In the first approximation of meaning in life, Schmid moves away from any higher, external or pre-defined purpose and states that the meaning of life, or to have a 'meaningful' life is to live a beautiful life, i.e., to make one's life

---

17 It also requires students to do their part to actualise flourishing, but this argument can be brought against any aims and ends of education.
18 Kristjánsson amends Aristotle's original point of 'needing to have children' here and follows Hursthouse's amended neo-Aristotelean position.

beautiful, which he defines as an 'affirmative life' [bejahenswertes Leben], a life one can say 'yes' to, or a life one considers worth living (p. 169). Returning to the Stephen Hawking's example to illustrate the point, it is conceivable that he might have looked back at his life and considered it a life worth living even though it has been a life of hardship and egregious health challenges. This take of meaning of life for Schmid then is distinct to, although supported by, the ability of *hermeneutics*: the ability of interpretation and sense making of what one experiences in life. Schmid (p. 294) states that we can only shape our life effectively towards a beautiful life if we can understand how 'things' in life interact and 'work'. Through interpretation of what we perceive and experience, we can make sense of life and understand how 'life works' and through this understanding find and define our own place in 'life', which arguably contributes to the sense of meaning and purpose in life as Kristjánsson explains it. As such, the art of living – and an education for the art of living – does not have 'a sense of meaning and purpose' as a necessary pre-requisite but *is* the deliberate action *to make sense* of life and *to find meaning* in life through shaping one's life into a beautiful life, a life worth living.

So, to conclude, I have shown in the above that, while the notion of flourishing and Schmid's concept of the art of living share common roots in Aristotelian thought, they are clearly distinct in their form (their essence) – one is a state of being, the other a process and way of life – as well as in their supposed pre-conditions. Flourishing is a somewhat more demanding concept in terms of potential achievement, Schmid's art of living is a more refined concept of how to purposefully shape one's life towards a life one considers worth living: a beautiful life. And while some very basic external pre-conditions for the engagement with an art of living exist (such as the ability to act, the means to survive on a daily basis, and the ability to make decisions in the first place), the faculties and knowledge areas to develop and engage in the art of living, however, can reasonably be placed within the purview of education. Therefore, I would argue that Schmid's concept of the art of living is a more fitting end of education than flourishing as it sits more closely within the realm of what education – as in teaching and learning, but also as knowledge and understanding – can actually *do* for human beings, which I have alerted to before and will discuss in more detail in the following chapter. The question that remains now is the relationship between human flourishing, the art of living and a beautiful life. While this relationship depends significantly on the definition of flourishing used, going back to Kristjánsson's definition above as the 'developmentally progressive activity of a meaningful ... life', I would argue that flourishing is what might happen while a person is engaged in the art of living and actively tries to shape their life into a beautiful life, what they consider a life worth living.

Conclusion

In his chapter, I have discussed the difference between short-lived, contextual, and varied external *aims in education* and a potential long-lived, overarching, and intrinsic *end of education* by exploring and clarifying the different meanings of the term 'education' and how it is used in the public and academic discourse. Drawing on the German notions of *Erziehung*, *Bildung* and *Entfaltung*, as well as R. S. Peters and John Dewey's work, I have argued that education ought to be understood as a holistic concept that is more than just a means to an end; rather it is an end in itself and that this end aligns with, if not is synonymous to, the development of students' own art of living. I have further discussed how this call for the art of living as the end of education is not sitting in isolation but aligns well with Biesta's concept of *world-centred education*. I argued that Biesta's work and my approach to education for an art of living are not only compatible but complimentary in their view towards 'good education' in schools, centres, and education systems. Finally, I discussed the relationship between *flourishing* and the art of living and argued that the latter makes for a better end of education due to its nature being more in line with what education can *do* rather than what education might *entail* if a range of other pre-conditions are met as well. In the following chapter, I will discuss what then it is that teachers, schools, and centres can do in their settings as an education for the art of living.

References

Biesta, G. (2013). *The beautiful risk of education*. Paradigm.
Biesta, G. (2022). *World-centred education: A view for the present*. Routledge.
Biesta, G. J. J. (2015). *Good education in an age of measurement: Ethics, politics, democracy, good education in an age of measurement: Ethics, politics, democracy*. doi:10.4324/9781315634319.
Brighouse, H. (2008). Education for a flourishing life. *Yearbook of the National Society for the Study of Education*, 107(1), 58–71. Available at: http://search.ebscohost.com.ezproxy.can terbury.ac.nz/login.aspx?direct=true&db=ehh&AN=34186970&site=ehost-live.
Dewey, J. (2008). Democracy and education 1916, by John Dewey. *Schools*, 5(1/2), 87–95. doi:10.1086/591813.

D'Olimpio, L., Gatley, J., & Wareham, R. (2024). *Philosophy of education*. Palgrave.
Foucault, M. (1984). *The care of the self*. London, England: Penguin Books (The history of sexuality).
Kristjánsson, K. (2012). Positive psychology and positive education: Old wine in new bottles?. *Educational Psychologist*, 47(2), 86–105. doi:10.1080/00461520.2011.610678.
Kristjánsson, K. (2019). *Flourishing as the aim of education, flourishing as the aim of education*. New York, NY: Routledge. doi:10.4324/9780429464898.
Liebau, E. (1999). *Erfahrung und Verantwortung. Werteerziehung als Pädagogik der Teilhabe*. Weinheim; München, Germany: Juventa.
MacIntyre, A. (1981). *After virtue: A study in moral theory*. London: Duckworth.
O'Neill, J. (2023). The degradation of teachers' work, loss of teachable moments, demise of democracy and ascendancy of surveillance capitalism in schooling. *New Zealand Journal of Teachers' Work*, 20(2), 179–189.
Peters, R. S. (1973). *Authority, responsibility and education*. New York, NY: Paul S. Eriksson.
de Ruyter, D. (2004). Pottering in the garden? On human flourishing and education. *Journal of Educational Studies*, 52(4), 377–389.
Schmid, W. (2000a). *Philosophie der Lebenskunst: Eine Grundlegung*. Frankfurt: Suhrkamp.
Schmid, W. (2000b). *Schönes Leben? Eine Einführung in die Lebenskunst*. Frankfurt, Germany: Suhrkamp.
Teschers. (2013). An educational approach to the art of living. *Knowledge Cultures*, 1(2), 25–32.
Teschers, C. (2017). A BEAUTIFUL LIFE AS AN END OF EDUCATION. *Knowledge Cultures*, 5(6), 62–73. doi:10.22381/KC5620175.
Teschers, C. (2018). *Education and Schmid's art of living, education and Schmid's art of living*. Routledge. doi:10.4324/9781315563848.
Teschers, C., Neuhaus, T., & Vogt, M. (2024). Troubling the boundaries of traditional schooling for a rapidly changing future – Looking back and looking forward. *Educational Philosophy and Theory*, (early online), 1–12. doi:10.1080/00131857.2024.2321932.
White, J. (2011). *Exploring well-being in schools: A guide to making children's lives more fulfilling*. Routledge.

· 6 ·

EDUCATION FOR AN ART OF LIVING

I have dedicated the previous chapters in this book mainly to the *why* and partly the *what* of the various aspects in which education and the art of living can come together, inform each other, support individuals and society in positive ways, and, in-fact, share a common end: to enable students to develop their own art of living in pursuit of a beautiful life. I will now turn the discussion towards the *how*, the actual implications for educational theory and practice in an education for an art of living. I will start with looking at selected current dominant strands in educational theory and practice from a comparative perspective – particularly considering the outcome focused competencies idea dominant in much of the English speaking discourse and the input focused notion of *Bildung* in the German (and some other European countries') tradition in relation to a holistic approach to education. Then, I will dive into implications and suggestions for curriculum and pedagogy in schooling contexts, before discussing if an education for an art of living can be achieved by reforming and tweaking what is already there or requires a more fundamental rethinking of schooling and education systems.

Education as Bildung vs. Competencies

In the context of education systems and their foundations, Autio (2021) provides an interesting overview and discussion of some of the differences between the US/UK education tradition, based on competencies and pre-defined learning outcomes, and the more continental European tradition, based on the German concept of *Bildung*, which takes a more holistic approach to the development of human beings as educated subjects. Autio writes in the wake of the PISA success of the Finish education system, which, he argues, ignored the competency focused agenda proposed by the OECD and instead followed a more humanistic approach in the Finish adaptation of the German *Bildung's* tradition. He strongly suggests that what we value in education as a society – such as equity, fairness, democracy, but also including what the economy and industry values expressed in PISA test results – is not readily supported by a limited focus of education on competencies and measurable outcomes but can be more successful if approached from a different, a more holistic and inclusive rather than competitive, conceptualisation of education. I will provide a quick overview of the history of competency-based learning, drawing on collaborative work with colleagues (Teschers, Neuhaus & Vogt, 2024), and then provide an argument that shows that the competency-based model of education, dominant in many English speaking countries, might not be well suited in their current form to support an education for an art of living, or any form of 'good education' (cf. Biesta, 2022) for that matter – at least in its extreme implementations.

Competency-based learning can be traced back to the *Sputnik shock* of 1957, which heavily influenced the political and military climate at the time in which the 'West', and most dominantly the US, aimed at 'winning' the technological race and Cold War with the then Soviet Union. Among others, this led to a reform of the education system at the time. Education was considered 'too important to be left to educators' and so a quality control system for high schools was proposed by a Navy admiral (cf. Vogt & Neuhaus, 2021) that aimed at breaking down subject content into assessable and measurable chunks, skills and competences. Since then, through lobbying work of the US, the *Scientist in the classroom* approach and 'the testing instruments which had been developed to evaluate competency-based learning's efficiency became the basis for modern-day PISA testing' (Teschers et al., 2024: 2) and have, over the last two decades, become akin to a global standard through global comparative testing regimes. In consequence, the US/UK competency-based approach to education has invaded many education systems internationally, including some Scandinavian countries (cf. Autio, 2021) and other European countries, such as Germany after the so-called *PISA shock* in 2000, as well as previously colonised countries such as Australia and New Zealand and beyond. The critique of *learnification* (Biesta, 2022), discussed in earlier chapters, touches on a similar note with Biesta's critique of the imbalance of today's education systems and schooling in their nearly exclusive emphasis on *qualification* (for industry and economy), rather than the holistic development of the human being for a better and more desirable society, which would be closer linked with the German *Bildung's* tradition.

It is interesting to note here that Germany, despite being the country of origin of the notion of *Bildung*, did not have similar outcomes in PISA testing as the Finish system had. While this is not the space to delve into a detailed comparison, Kricke (2010) shows that the inclusive school approach in Finland seems to be a generally more desirable implementation in line with relevant values proposed within *Bildung* than the streamed approach implemented in Germany, utilising a three-tiered system – a notion that is similarly supported by Autio (2021). It seems that the more inclusive school system in Finland, with a school-for-all approach, is not only perceived as more equitable but also has better outcomes for students in academic achievement. Interestingly, New Zealand has taken a mixed approach, utilising a similar inclusive school-for-all approach (and scoring better on international rankings than Germany, although not as high as Finland), but having followed a more prescribed learning outcomes and competencies approach rather than a holistic approach to *Bildung*. Although a moderating factor in the New Zealand context can be found in the bi-cultural history of the country and the endeavour to include more holistic indigenous values and approaches in education, which arguably have closer links to *Bildung* than to competencies[1]. However, this focus on competencies arguably has increased since PISA testing was introduced and the relatively broad and flexible New Zealand Curriculum of 2007 has been partly undermined by external learning outcomes, such as National Standards that were introduced by the National led government in 2010 but scrapped again by a Labour led government in 2018. Interestingly, a drop in PISA achievement in New Zealand coincides with the introduction of National Standards and student achievement continues to decline since. However, New Zealand is still operating above OECD average, which is a relieve to us living here (OECD, 2023). As such, I find New Zealand an interesting

---

1 A current research project I am running with colleagues in parallel while writing this book is exploring the relationships between *Bildung*, the Māori notion of *Ako* (teaching & learning), and competence-based education approaches. While none of these approaches can be seen as synonymous, initial findings suggest a closer link and more overlap between *ako* and *Bildung* than between either of them with the competence-based education tradition. This said, *ako* seems to sit slightly 'closer' towards competence models than *Bildung*, if we consider these terms as part of a continuum. The overlap between *Bildung* and competencies is arguably rather slim, although some authors try to force an artificial link that seems to bend these concepts 'out of shape' to make them fit.

experiment that tries to integrate an education system arguably based on egalitarian and inclusive education values, steered largely by neoliberal and economic (OECD) ideologies, although balanced somewhat through efforts by academics and educators (as well as some politicians) to integrate indigenous values that juxtapose these currently dominant ideologies. Dominant notions of individualism, competition and unchecked growth and exploitation of resources are moderated by indigenous values in favour of community, collaboration, sustainability, and stewardship of resources. It seems therefore, that the New Zealand system sits somewhat in the middle between extreme forms of competency driven and *Bildung* driven approaches to education. What is pertinent from this excursus for our topic at hand is that seemingly, inclusive schooling settings that take a more holistic approach to human development can fare better on both economic and humanistic outcome attributes for students and society, even if impacted by neoliberally driven ideologies promoting competencies and outcome driven schooling practices.

Returning to the comparison at hand, following Bernd Lederer's (2014: 39–41) distinction between two key concepts in the German education discourse, *Bildung* (self-formation, self-cultivation) and *Erziehung* (raising, upbringing), it seems that competency-focused education is closer aligned with the ideas behind *Erziehung*. Lederer explains, drawing on Helmwart Hierdeis' work, that, despite some overlap between the two concepts, *Erziehung* refers more closely to the process of supporting a less experienced or knowledgeable person (i.e., child/youth/student) to rise to the level of the more experienced or knowledgeable person (i.e., adult/teacher) through direction, instruction, facilitation, motivation, and other activities that are akin to pedagogy. *Bildung*, on the other hand, can be seen as the result of a largely self-directed engagement of the individual with the world through, for example, language, literature, science, art and media that transforms information into knowledge that is relevant for the individual in their relationship with the world. *Erziehung* sees the individual as 'lacking' or missing in their development and aims towards enabling a person to become a functioning member of society. While *Bildung* is to a point dependent on *Erziehung*, it reaches beyond towards '*Selbstdenken, Selbstbestimmung und Selbstaneignung*' [thinking for oneself, self-determination and self-formation] (2014: 40–41) and is as such a never-ending process of self-formation and self-cultivation. Competency-based education, as described above, seems to align much more closely with the basics of *Erziehung* and seems to aim towards shaping a student into a functioning subject of society with a focus on supporting industry and economy first, while other values are subordinate to these. As such, I want to argue, competency-based education falls short of supporting human beings in their development as self-thinking, self-determined and self-forming agents and rather supports a development as functioning entities, not unlike the process of equipping machines (e.g., robots, AI, etc.) with certain skills to perform needed tasks. While this comparison is certainly a bit overstated, I hope to illustrate the underlying view of students as 'lacking' and in need of upskilling to be a 'useful' member of society, rather than a view of students as individual human beings with a range of aptitudes that can be nurtured to support a rounded and holistic development of personhood. It is not surprising that subjects and disciplines like the arts and humanities are often somewhat under threat in neoliberally driven competency-based education systems. Arguably, competency-based education might also pose a threat to democracy and democratic citizenship, as democratic citizens are expected to be able to understand the wider complexities of the world and the political sphere to make sensible decisions in enacting their civil duties and rights (e.g., voting, advocating, etc.), in line with their self-reflected norms, values and beliefs. I am unconvinced that a pure competency-based model of education can deliver on these aspects sufficiently.

Returning to the notion of *Bildung* as alternative driver for educational practice and schooling, Autio (2021) refers to this tradition, arguing that the inclusive school model in Finland is based on the original humanistic idea of *Bildung*. Besides the inclusive and equity aspects that a *Bildung* approach to education can have, a focus on the 'educated subject' (Autio, 2021) rather than the competent worker/employee also links with other humanistic aspirations relevant to (democratic) societies, such as a broader understanding of the world and its interconnections locally and globally – a faculty that arguably is fundamental to a well-functioning democracy that requires its citizens to make sensible decisions about their leadership and representation, as discussed above. On a confronting note, one might wonder if a competency focus in public schooling over decades might have contributed to the flood and success of populist propaganda and hard to fathom voting patters in many democratic countries today. Certainly, the outpour of hatred, racism, segregation, nationalism and the prevalence of wars today has many causes and contributing factors, and education cannot solve these issues alone (even though education seems often to be expected to 'fix' all evils in the world); however, it seems pertinent to ask what contribution education can make to help humanity to improve globally and, as Dewey (2008: 100) stated, become 'the best possible realization of humanity as humanity'. A holistic approach to education through *Bildung* and the *educated subject* equipped for a life-long journey of personal development seems more promising than a technicist approach towards competencies education and finite learning outcomes. After all, learning and human development does not stop once a defined 'learning outcome' has been achieved.

Curriculum and Pedagogy for an Art of Living

Bildung and the educated subject is also a key aspect of Schmid's art of living. *Bildung* understood as well-rounded humanistic education that enables the subject engaged in the art of living to see the interconnections in the world and enact effective change is a cornerstone of shaping one's own life actively. The educated subject, who is able to grow and develop as a human being, reflect on their own norms, values and beliefs, and shape their actions and habits [Schmid: *Gestik*] accordingly, and who has an understanding of what is the right thing to do (*phronésis*) is much more likely and able to actively take responsibility for their own life and shape it into a beautiful life, rather than being driven by external expectations and become an unthinking (learning) machine without agency (cf. Biesta, 2020). But what is needed to equip people to become educated subjects able to develop their own art of living? What content is necessary or relevant, and how can it or should it be taught, which pedagogy employed? I will offer suggestions here that will form a partial answer to these questions, although no answer will be complete in any way due to the contextual nature of human life and interaction in educational settings (cf. Schmid, 2000: 311–312; Biesta, 2015).

At the centre of an educational response to the art of living is Schmid's notion of *life-knowledge* [Lebenwissen] – knowledge pertaining to the *know-how* of life: how to live, how to navigate (everyday) life, understanding the working and interconnections of human life and being in the world (cf. Schmid, 2000: 297–303). Schmid distinguishes purposefully the concept of life-knowledge (knowledge *of* and *for* life) from a more scientific approach of knowledge *about* life [Lebenswissen]. While Schmid does not want to diminish the importance of academic[2] knowledge areas and subjects, he emphasises

---

2 I use 'academic' here to include the different disciplines grouped under 'sciences' and 'humanities' in English (which would both sit under the 'science' umbrella in German) in an attempt to be inclusive and give equal importance to all disciplines.

life-knowledge as distinct to point out that it is just as important (if not more so) for human beings to be able to live a good and beautiful life. Arguably, knowledge about things and the world, as in the domain of academic exploration and research, are important for life-knowledge in terms of understanding the interconnections in the world: understanding how things work, so that one can identify the leavers of change relevant to one's pursuit of a beautiful life. Schmid (2000: 309), however, emphasises that a hermeneutical interpretative step [hermeneutische Anstrengung] is needed to make abstract academic knowledge relevant to the life of the individual in form of life-knowledge. Schmid proposes *philosophy* as one way to support this hermeneutical process, which I will comment on further below. In terms of life-knowledge domains, in an interview with Schmid (Neuhaus, Schmid & Vogt, 2023), he suggested these examples: nutrition and food (how to stay healthy and look after oneself), economy and finances (relevance of one's skills and abilities, and the role of one's own job in the bigger picture of one's life), shopping (what is relevant/ necessary/ appropriate? What is not?), decision making (how to make sensible decisions; strategic thinking), programming and technology (understanding technology and algorithms), and the workings of science (understanding how knowledge formation and science works, what the limitations are, and how to distinguish 'facts' from fiction). These examples, while clearly relevant to the particular cultural and historical context in which the interview took place, provide insights into the kind of topics that can be grouped under life-knowledge for the development of an art of living. The concrete content, however, needs to be carefully considered based on the local context and the lived and experienced reality [Lebenswirklichkeit] of students, teachers, and the surrounding community. These content areas are mostly quite tangible and practical, and surely partially covered in educational settings to some extent. Also, calls for nutrition and financial literacy to become part of the curriculum as important 'skills' for people to live successfully have been voiced occasionally over time in different contexts. However, one would be hard pressed to find an education setting (maybe outside of early childhood education) that includes a deliberate approach towards including life-knowledge, as described here, in its curriculum and practice.

In a related manner, William Pinar (2011, 2022) questions the role of traditional curriculum in favour of a form of 'lived curriculum', which he terms *currere*. Pinar explains currere as a form of active and subjective engagement with content (information, knowledge, experiences) in a reflective manner that brings together one's lived past and ones expectations for the future in the present to support understanding of content matter in relation to oneself. Through four steps of (i) returning to the past, (ii) imagining the future, (iii) the analytical moment through study, and (iv) the synthetic phase, the individual engages not in a mere 'learning' of content but in a transformative process of becoming and re-formation of self – a process that arguably relates closely to the German notion of *Bildung* as (trans-) formation of the self and Biesta's (2022) notion of subjectification. Currere, Pinar (2022: 2) explains, emphasises the lived curriculum but also acknowledges the planned curriculum. However, he cautions that an institutionalised planned curriculum aimed at fulfilling institutional measures rather than focusing on the formation and becoming of the educated subject can indeed risk 'erasing the subjective sphere' (2022: 3). A lived curriculum, on the other hand, is linked to lived experiences of teachers' and students' past, present and future and emphasises the everyday experiences of the individual, not only through busy study, but also through phases of silence, contemplation and reflection. So, bringing together Schmid's focus on life-knowledge and Pinar's notion of currere, one call for schools and education systems would be to take a more deliberate approach towards developing a lived curriculum and including life-knowledge in their curriculum and teaching practices. How these can be implemented, however, is a different matter and I will discuss later in this chapter how school and education can be thought of differently, and maybe ought to be thought of differently.

Continuing with content and curriculum considerations in terms of education for an art of living, I listed in the previous chapter already themes Schmid proposed: '*the human being as individual; the social human being; difficulties and burdens of human life; striving for fulfilment and meaning in life; religions, beliefs and cultures of humanity; and the personal shape of one's life and global perspectives*' (Teschers, 2017: 69–70; italics in original). As indicated earlier, these themes are not to be taken as complete but are rather intended as additional to more traditional academic school subject areas, which are certainly also important for one's understanding of the world, as well as one's ability to qualify for a job to support oneself financially – what Biesta would call the *qualification* purpose of education. While schools seem to place emphasis strongly on the qualification aspect, what Schmid's list of themes adds, as discussed elsewhere (Teschers et al., 2024), sits arguably more in Biesta's (2022) *socialisation* and *subjectification* purposes of education. As such, the proposed themes support to balance curricula and schooling approaches, as Biesta calls for, towards a more holistic approach to human development, including the becoming of an active agent in the world. In addition to Schmid's list, together with colleagues I proposed three additional themes with an eye on life-knowledge that also seem relevant and important enough to warrant their own mentioning: 'economic structures of human societies; legal, political and governmental organisation of human co-existence; and [...] science, technology and the arts of humanity' (Teschers et al., 2024: 7). While some of these themes might overlap in aspects with Schmid's list above, I consider these important areas of knowledge to understand some of the leavers of power and structures necessary for individuals to be able to consider effective change in economic and political contexts. The theme of 'science, technology and the arts' links with Schmid's interview examples of understanding programming and algorithms, for example, to understand how computers, social media and technology influence our thinking and engagement with information and each other. However, we deliberately included 'the arts' to emphasise that science and technology, which is often the focus of school curricula following the 'scientist in the classroom' tradition as explained above, are not enough for a well-rounded holistic (some might call it 'liberal') education. I will comment below how, for example philosophy and art education, are relevant for people to develop their own art of living.

One important consideration for curriculum development in regards to the art of living, Schmid (2000: 311–312) points out, has to be that content cannot be *normative* but has to be *optative*: in an education for the art of living, we cannot prescribe a canon that has to be taught, but only (in the tradition of *Bildung*) lay out the vast breadth of relevant knowledge and allow the student to select the areas that are of most importance to them (cf. Pinar, 2022). However, the breadth of knowledge on offer, according to Schmid (2000: 312), needs to include not only academic knowledge that can be of relevance, but also hermeneutical knowledge that allows a critical engagement with knowledge and information, and knowledge pertaining to the 'know-how' of life, *life-knowledge*, with a more immediate focus on everyday life in local and global contexts. To enable the child (or adolescent) to make a sensible selection, requires, however, the development of phronésis [Klugheit] – i.e., the understanding of what is necessary, relevant, and important for oneself to know and develop – to support the individual to engage in such knowledge areas in the pursuit of their own beautiful life (ibid.). Such an open approach to pedagogy, without narrowly defined learning outcomes and a rather broad range of developmental pathways, I would argue does not align well with a competency approach to education as discussed earlier. As such, education systems that are based on the mantra of compartmentalised competencies and broken-down skills and knowledge packages require some re-consideration if the development of an art of living and a beautiful life should become the focus of the educational endeavour (which I am arguing for in this book). How this might happen, I will consider further in the next section. However, first I need to touch on pedagogy and classroom practice.

To start, I will return to the point Schmid made proposing philosophy as one possible approach to provide students with the hermeneutical understanding to transfer academic knowledge into life-knowledge relevant to their own context. What can be helpful in this context is the philosophical method of critical reflection, interpretation and analytical consideration. One way to practice these faculties can be through the pedagogical approach of *Communities of (philosophical) Inquiry* (CoI), as proposed by Lipman and Sharp under the umbrella of Philosophy for Children (P4C). While Lipman and Sharp proposed an elaborate set of texts that can be contemplated with students using CoIs as a method, CoIs can also be used to address all sorts of questions with students using philosophical practices[3]. Millett and Tapper (2012) have summarised some of the positive impacts that the use of CoIs can have for students, beyond gaining a deeper understanding of the topic at hand, and reemphasise the development of the '4C's' often cited in the context of P4C: the strengthening of *critical, caring, creative,* and *collaborative* thinking skills. In earlier work with Laura D'Olimpio, we have discussed in more detail how P4C and particularly CoIs can be conducive to the development of students' own art of living (D'Olimpio & Teschers, 2017). Main contributing factors include the honing of the hermeneutical abilities to critically and creatively consider how academic knowledge can become relevant for the pursuit and shaping of one's own beautiful life. The creative element supports individuals to envision new and original ways of living and shaping their lives rather than simply adopting existing examples of how one could live (Schmid, 2000: 313). Schmid argues further that through the creative element and engagement with the arts, and art in form of drawing, music and others, students can practice how to give form to something new, which then

---

3 A CoI can be pictures as a loose circle of students and one or more teachers in which the teacher becomes the facilitator of a discussion on a question or topic. Knowledge und understanding is co-created by the group rather than offered by the teacher/facilitator. Hypothesis offered are critically examined by the group in a respectful and collaborative manner and tested regarding their plausibility. See, for example, D'Olimpio and Teschers (2017) for a more detailed description.

can be applied to the shaping of their own life, and, in the process, contributes to the shaping of their own self, which is the inherent process of *Bildung* [self-formation], but also resonates with the becoming of a self in Biesta's (2022) notion of *subjectification*. The caring and collaborative thinking skills fostered through CoIs can further support the development of an enlightened self-interest through *phronêsis* and encourage each individual engaged in the art of living, through guided reflection, to create an environment that is conducive to the development of an art of living for each member of a community and/or society. I have already discussed the implications for the wellbeing of individuals and society in Chapter Three.

However, although I focused so far on philosophy as a method, philosophy *in* schools, i.e., the engagement with traditional philosophy either through CoIs or other means, can further support the students' deeper understanding of what is necessary, relevant and important in life and for their own life. Therefore, including traditional philosophy in school curricula, which I included implicitly (philosophers may forgive me) in my emphasis of the relevance of the arts in the curriculum, will further support students' ability to make sense of the world and transfer abstract academic knowledge into relevant life-knowledge for one's own art of living. This said, philosophy can also play a particularly strong role in reflecting on norms, values and beliefs one is exposed to by society, parents and peers, and help shape one's own self and view of the world. As such, philosophy itself can be a powerful contributor to the formation and shaping of one's self and the direction one envisions for one's own beautiful life.

Returning to pedagogy in the classroom, while CoIs have been offered here as a pedagogical method to strengthen relevant thinking skills and faculties for the development of an art of living, not that much can be said beyond the usual about how teachers should engage their students. Much of the process of teaching and learning is contextual to the local situation, students, teachers, cultural background and local communities involved. As Biesta (2015) explains, there is no hard-and-fast rule about best practices in education. We cannot say 'what works' in education, but only 'what *has* worked' at a particular time, with particular students and teachers, in a particular setting. And while some pedagogical methods might have more potential than others, no one approach will always be the right one. What remains on offer, however, is to remind us that for the development of an art of living, it is important to understand the interconnections in the world. For this, it is important to understand 'things' in the broader context and in relation to one's own experienced life-reality [Lebenswirklichkeit]. Therefore, Schmid emphasises the importance of integrating new knowledge, may it be life-knowledge or academic knowledge, into the bigger picture of one's life and the world. Using themes that permeate different subject areas and allow the connection of specific subject knowledge to a larger topic with clear relevance to students' current and/or future life would be one way of addressing this. For example, a topic of interest to students might be if a new cycleway could be built to allow safer access to the school for students. This could be approached from a health and physical education perspective; from a sociological and governmental perspective regarding city planning, petition processes and other aspects; in geology a possible route could be analysed regarding the implications of landscape and ground formation, etc.; in math all sorts of calculations can be attached to such a project; and in language education, petition letters or other forms of communication could be practiced, to name only a few ideas[4]. Schmid also suggests the method of role-play, which could be particularly helpful in arts and social science topics to support the subjectification and socialisation purposes of education in schools to address, for example, themes such as *the human being as individual* and *the social human being*.

Beyond the pedagogy in the classroom, Schmid further mentioned the importance of authentic engagement with real world experts and contexts. For example, to learn about different religions of the world, instead of merely reading about them, a visit to local places of prayer and practice, as well as meeting practitioners and spiritual leaders (e.g., imams, kohen, priests) could bring these to life and support understanding and tolerance through experience and exposure. Similarly, visits to botanic gardens and local experts can support students' learning in biology about local and global flora and fauna. In the Aotearoa New Zealand context, considering our bi-cultural heritage alerted to earlier in this book, authentic connection with mana whenua (the ancestral Māori people of the land) can support place-based learning (cf. Penetito, 2009) and meaningful visits to local marae (Māori meeting places), to provide an example form the current local context in which this book is written. Much more could be said in this space, and I am certain, practicing teachers can find much better examples in their local contexts, but I hope that my musings here exemplify possibilities and how these real-world connections

---

[4] I apologise to subject teachers for my rather rudimentary understanding of your respective areas but hope that these considerations exemplify suitably the possibilities of using overarching themes across distinct subject matters.

can make a difference for students to understand the relevance of knowledge for their own context and development of an art of living.

Reform vs. Revolution of Schooling

Having contemplated some of the history of schooling, the complexity between *Bildung* and competency approaches to education and schooling, and some of the implications and suggestions for curriculum and pedagogy, the question arises if we can tweak existing education systems to accommodate enough of these aspects and re-focus schools towards the development of students' own art of living, or if this might require a more fundamental overhaul of the system? Even though I started this book stating that I would argue for a shift in education, during the year writing this book, continuing research, and discussing aspects of my work with various colleagues, I am not that certain anymore that a shift is sufficient or possible at all. In my recent work with Michaela Vogt and Till Neuhaus from Bielefeld University (Germany), I was reminded of the notion of the 'grammar of schooling' (Tyack & Tobin, 1994). Prof. Vogt, an expert in the history of education and *Bildung*, and I contemplated how schools and education systems undergo nearly constant reforms of the one or other aspect of the system, but that by and large the underlying principles and workings of schools and education systems have not changed significantly in any meaningful way (cf. Tyack & Tobin, 1994; see also Teschers et al., 2024). As such it is questionable if tweaking or 'reforming' aspects of education systems and schooling can indeed bring us to the point where the holistic development of human beings as human beings and the development of their own art of living will become the focus, as I have argued in Chapter Five and throughout this book.

The answer to this question, as so often in education, will depend to a point on the respective context and national education system we are looking at. I mentioned the Finish system above and Autio's discussion around their arguably more holistic *Bildung* approach, paired with an inclusive school model, which might lend itself more to tweaking or small reforms, rather than a revolution of the system. Other systems that seem to strongly stratify students, are exclusive by design to some or many, and/or are strongly based on a narrow competence approach, focused on science and technology qualification skills, might need to be reconsidered more fundamentally. The answer for any particular context will require a somewhat detailed evaluation of the education system and curricula in place, as well as a review of common pedagogy and classroom practices, in relation to how an education for a beautiful life would look like. Work on this question is currently ongoing and will be the topic of future publications. However, there are some guiding questions and principles I can offer to date that can help in this context.

In recent work with colleagues, we have proposed two guiding questions for the evaluation of any system or context in relation to the art of living: '*what is necessary to support students (in our local context) to develop their own art of living?*' and in relation to existing settings and curriculum, '*is this content/practice directly supportive for the development of our students' own art of living?*' (Teschers et al., 2024: 5–6, italics in original). For the first question, further refinement and criteria can be provided based on the content of this and other chapters in this book. First, (i) fundamental for the art of living is the development of self – Biesta's notion of *subjectification* – the development of agency. As such, the 2nd question could be restated as: is the way education and schooling is structured in the local context supportive of developing students' agency and self-hood, or is more targeted towards (unquestioning) discipline and acceptance of content on offer? This question would permeate all levels from how the system and schools are organised, how pedagogy and the role of the teacher is understood (e.g., 'sage on the stage' vs a 'guide' to support personal development and growths), and how the curriculum is made up and presented. Secondly, (ii) *phronésis* [Klugheit; prudence and practical wisdom] is a key faculty to transform self-centredness into, what Schmid calls, enlightened self-interest (Biesta's corresponding term would be world-centredness) that allows to see oneself in relation to others and the world and understand the complex interconnections between oneself and the world[5]. Further, (iii) the relevant curriculum needs to be considered in relation to the proposed themes listed earlier in this chapter. However, the relevant content that goes under each of these themes needs to be carefully considered based on the national and local context, as mentioned earlier. And (iv), pedagogy and teaching practices need to be considered in relation to these aspects mentioned here and above, such as allowing students to select (with scaffolding and support) which areas of knowledge are most important for them, and providing flexibility in what to study, and how. As an educator passionate about equity and inclusions, aspects of universal design for learning (Meyer, Rose & Gordon, 2014), inclusive pedagogy practices (e.g., Ballard, 2012; Teschers, 2020), as

---

5 On how to teach and evaluate *phronésis* in school contexts, see for example Kristjánsson (2015, 2019).

well as culturally responsive pedagogy (MacFarlane, 2004; Macfarlane et al., 2012) come to mind. However, all of these are relevant for good teaching and educational practices independent of the art of living as a focus. This said, they are crucial in the context of the art of living as aim of education and schooling as, through the ethics of the art of living (see Chapter Four), equity and social justice are inherent to any meaningful approach in this context.

Calls for substantial reform or even a revolution in education are not new. Dewey (1938), for example, advocated for different ways of engaging students, a different form of pedagogy but also a reconceptualisation of schooling and teaching around experience rather than rote learning and 'bookish' learning *about* the world. Maria Montessori (Raapke, 2006), Rudolf Steiner (Edmunds, 1987), A. S. Neill (Neill, 1992) and other actors of the progressive school movement envisioned alternative approaches to what was common practice in schools at the time. Some of these elements have found their way into mainstream schooling in some countries – although mostly reluctantly and with much delay. Key progressive aspects, such as allowing children to choose their own activities (Montessori), schooling without grades (Steiner), and democratic school communities that allow students similar consultation and voice as teachers and others (Summerhill/Neill), are still largely absent in mainstream schools. Still, many of the schools following a progressive framework are largely successful and often favoured by the rich and parents with higher levels of education, thus arguably continuing the inequities and structurally stratification of society through education systems as a whole. This divide between mainstream and project schools seems to me a systematic 'tinkering around the edges' rather than a full-scale review and change to the system at large, which resonates with Tyack and Tobin's (1994) persistent *grammar of schooling* argument. On a more radical note, Illich (1972) and Buckman (1973), for example, argued in the 1970s for the need of a more rigorous change to schooling in the so-called *de-schooling* movement. Among others, a more flexible approach to education over a person's lifetime and the de-centring of schools as the main (or only) place to acquire relevant knowledge, education, skills and qualifications was called for (cf. Teschers, 2018). This aligns to some extend with traditional indigenous approaches to education that were not necessarily bound to a building or a set time, for example (cf. Hemara, 2000).

While I do not want to argue here that any or all of these alternatives to current mainstream schools would be better suited to an education for the art of living, it is very likely that elements of these different streams can inform how an actual education aiming towards the development of students' own art of living could look like. As such, I would argue that even if we end up considering a revolution to be more likely to create an equitable education system than tinkering around the edges, it is very possible that the building blocks for a better system have already been developed and thought through. The work that lies ahead for interested researchers and academics in this area would be to consider what is already on offer and what would make most sense and provide the most likely support for the development of students' own art of living through education in centres and schools.

Conclusion

In this chapter, I considered some of the limitations of current education systems and schooling approaches, particularly such based on a competency framework. I argued that a *Bildung* approach to education shows more promise to be aligned with the holistic development of human beings, including being more responsive for the individual pathways people will embark on in their pursuit of a beautiful life through the development of their own art of living. The main purpose of this chapter has been to move my philosophical argument that education should aim towards the development of students' own art of living closer to the practice of teaching and schooling. In addition to curriculum themes and content areas that represent *life-knowledge* and are of particular relevance for an art of living, I proposed *Communities of (philosophical) Inquiry* as a pedagogical method that not only allows engagement with particular topics, but also supports the development of relevant thinking skills, such as *critical, creative, caring,* and *collaborative* thinking in the tradition of the Philosophy for Children. Other suggestions, such as authentic exposure and engagement with content in real life rather than the classroom only, as well as overarching themes that connect distinct academic subject content with each other and real-world scenarios relevant to students have been proposed. In the final section of this chapter, I pondered the question if an education for students' own art of living and pursuit of a beautiful life can be achieved through (yet another) reform to existing education systems and school approaches, or if a more fundamental redevelopment of (particularly mainstream) schooling might be necessary. While no distinct answer can be given here at this point, suggestions have been made how to evaluate national and local systems and individual school and centre settings in how well they do, and, indeed, are set up to support the development of students' own art of living. As final point, I proposed that even if a more fundamental re-thinking of schooling might be in order, the richness of the educational debate over the last 100 odd years likely holds many building blocks that can help us to create a better system and schools that are better equipped to support equity, fairness and justice, and the development of every student's own art of living and beautiful life.

References

Autio, T. (2021). From Knowledge and Bildung Toward Competences and Skills in Finnish Curriculum Policy?: Some Theoretical, Historical, and Current Observations Related to Finland. *Euro-Asian Encounters on 21st-Century Competency-Based Curriculum Reforms: Cultural Views on Globalization and Localization*, 41–56. doi:10.1007/978-981-16-3009-5_3/COVER.

Ballard, K. (2012). Inclusion and social justice: Teachers as agents of change. In S. Carrington & J. MacArthur (Eds.), *Teaching in inclusive school communities* (pp. 65–87). Milton: John Wiley & Sons.

Biesta, G. (2020). Can the prevailing description of educational reality be considered complete? On the Parks-Eichmann paradox, spooky action at a distance and a missing dimension in the theory of education. *Policy Futures in Education*, 18(8). doi:10.1177/1478210320910312.

Biesta, G. (2022). *World-centred education: A view for the present.* Routledge.

Biesta, G. J. J. (2015). Good education in an age of measurement: Ethics, politics, democracy, good education in an age of measurement: Ethics, politics, democracy. doi:10.4324/9781315634319.

Buckman, P. (1973). *Education without schools.* Edited by P. Buckman. London, England: Souvenir Press.

Dewey, J. (1938). *Experience and education.* New York, NY: Collier.

Dewey, J. (2008). Democracy and education 1916, by John Dewey. *Schools*, 5(1/2), 87–95. doi:10.1086/591813.

D'Olimpio, L., & Teschers, C. (2017). Playing with philosophy: Gestures, life-performance, P4C and an art of living. *Educational Philosophy and Theory*, 49(13), 1257–1266. doi:10.1080/00131857.2017.1294974.

Edmunds, Francis. (1987). *Rudolf Steiner education : The Waldorf school.* Rev. ed. London : Rudolf Steiner Press,.

Hemara, W. (2000). *Māori Pedagogies: A view from the literature.* NZCER.

Illich, I. D. (1972). *Deschooling society.* London, England: Calder \& Boyars.

Kricke, M. (2010). *Lernen und Lehren in Deutschland und Finnland-eine empirische Studie zu Schulsystem und LehrerInnenbil-dung im Ländervergleich Inauguraldissertation zur Erlangung des Doktorgrades.* Universität Köln.

Kristjánsson, K. (2015). *Aristotelian character education.* Routledge.

Kristjánsson, K. (2019). *Flourishing as the aim of education, flourishing as the aim of education.* New York, NY: Routledge. doi:10.4324/9780429464898.

Lederer, B. (2014). *Kompetenz oder Bildung.* Thesis Series. Innsbruck University Press. Available at: https://tuprints.ulb.tu-darmstadt.de/7177/1/Bildung%20-%20Wissen%20-%20Kompetenz.pdf (Accessed: 2 April 2024).

MacFarlane, A. (2004). *Kia hiwa ra! Listen to culture – Māori students' plea to educators.* Wellington, New Zealand: NZCER.

Macfarlane, A. et al. (2012). Inclusive education and Maori communities in Aotearoa New Zealand. In *Teaching in inclusive school communities.*

Meyer, A., Rose, D. H., & Gordon, D. T. (2014). *Universal design for learning : Theory and practice* (pp. 1–234).

Millett, S., & Tapper, A. (2012). Benefits of collaborative philosophical inquiry in schools. *Educational Philosophy and Theory,* 44(5), 546–567. doi:10.1111/j.1469-5812.2010.00727.x.

Neill, A. S. (1992). *The new Summerhill.* Edited by A. Lamb. London, England: Penguin Books.

Neuhaus, T., Schmid, W., & Vogt, M. (2023). *Kamiengespräch 2 mit Wilhelm Schmid über Motivation zur Lebenskunst und pädagogische Bezüge, AoL-Education project website.* Available at: http://aol-education.org/videos/ (Accessed: 20 March 2024).

OECD. (2023). *New Zealand | Factsheets | OECD PISA 2022 results.* Available at: https://www.oecd.org/publication/pisa-2022-results/country-notes/new-zealand-33941739/ (Accessed: 6 March 2024).

Penetito, W. (2009). Place-based education: Catering for curriculum, culture and community. *New Zealand annual review of education Te arotake a tau o te ao o te matauranga i Aotearoa,* 18, 5–29. Available at: https://ndhadeliver.natlib.govt.nz/delivery/DeliveryManagerServlet?dps_pid=FL2345846# (Accessed: 9 April 2024).

Pinar, W. (2022). *A praxis of presence in curriculum theory.* Routledge.

Pinar, W. F. (2011). *The character of curriculum studies.* New York: Palgrave Macmillan US. doi:10.1057/9781137015839.

Raapke, H.-D. (2006). *Montessori heute. Eine moderne Pädagogik für Familie, Kindergarten und Schule.* Hamburg, Germany: Rowohlt Taschenbuch Verlag.

Schmid, W. (2000). *Philosophie der Lebenskunst: Eine Grundlegung.* Frankfurt: Suhrkamp.

Teschers, C. (2017). A BEAUTIFUL LIFE AS AN END OF EDUCATION. *Knowledge Cultures,* 5(6), 62–73. doi:10.22381/KC5620175.

Teschers, C. (2018). *Education and Schmid's art of living, education and Schmid's art of living.* Routledge. doi:10.4324/9781315563848.

Teschers, C. (2020). Proposing a Holistic Inclusive Education Model for Policy, Curriculum and Classroom Development. *Teachers' Work,* 17 (1and 2), 73–87. doi:10.24135/teacherswork.v17i1and2.299.

Teschers, C., Neuhaus, T., & Vogt, M. (2024). 'Troubling the boundaries of traditional schooling for a rapidly changing future – Looking back and looking forward. *Educational Philosophy and Theory,* (early online), 1–12. doi:10.1080/00131857.2024.2321932.

Tyack, D., & Tobin, W. (1994). The "Grammar" of schooling: Why has it been so hard to change?. *American Educational Research Journal,* 31(3), 453–479. doi:10.3102/00028312031003453.

Vogt, M., & Neuhaus, T. (2021). Fachdidaktiken im Spannungsfeld zwischen kompetenzorientiertem fachlichen Lernen und inklusiver Pädagogik: Vereinigungsbemühungen oder Verdeckungsgeschehen?. *Zeitschrift für Grundschulforschung 2021*, *14*(1), 113–128. doi:10.1007/S42278-020-00093-5.

· 7 ·

CONCLUDING THOUGHTS – GOOD EDUCATION IN A CHANGING WORLD

In this final chapter, I would like to return to considerations of our changing world and some of the implications I see for education and teaching in schools and centres with an eye on practitioners. It seems to me that schools and teaching practice can easily become trapped between constant change and more of the same. Especially in smaller countries, like New Zealand, where much of the policy direction and top-down requirements can change on the whim of the government, schools, centres and teachers are often faced with significant changes and requirements to aspects of their work, while the education system and the overall 'grammar of schooling' (Tyack & Tobin, 1994) of how schools operate remain largely the same. One example might be the aforementioned National Standards, which had a significant impact on what has been taught and how it has been reported on to government and parents, but had arguably little impact on the quality of how teachers teach their students in the classroom in particular, or how schools and centres are organised[1]. About 10 years later, the National Standards were abolished (by a change of government) and teachers asked to return to the National Curriculum (a

---

1   Although an impact on, for example, 'teaching to the test', and limitations of how to work within the New Zealand Curriculum might have been some factors driven by the National Standards Framework.

more flexible document than the standards) as their main guide for teaching. A recent change in government now seems to suggest that a more structured curriculum might be on the cards that is a bit more prescriptive to what is taught in each year group. Also, structured literacy has been mandated for all schools as a one-size-fits-all approach and schools must comply from the beginning of next year. These developments equate to much back and forth and constant change for teachers. Another example has been the shift to flexible learning environments (FLE) in New Zealand in the 2010s. Many buildings had to be changed, classes regrouped and teachers had to teach collaboratively larger groups than single-cell classrooms. Arguably, one of the most substantial shifts around how teaching took place in this country in recent years (Benade, 2017; Patrix & Benade, 2018). This said, not enough support was given to teachers to reconceptualise how they teach and what pedagogies they employ in these new spaces and configurations (Benade, 2019). And so, in many instances, teaching did not change that much and teachers and students just tried to make things work in larger, noisier and sometimes more chaotic environments. In personal communication with teachers in one school with purpose built flexible learning environments, it was suggested that teachers worked strategically to create the resemblance of single-cell classrooms teaching and use the space creatively in a way that reduces noise and allows more traditional instruction and engagement with students. Another example is a local high school that was also a new build during the time of the FLE hype and which just this year has decided to refurbish the open space back into single-cell environments as teaching and learning was just not working as well as initially hoped for. So, much has changed, back and forth, and much energy and effort been used, but in the end, one could argue that not much has changed at all.

However, the foundations of our schooling system and how schools operate reaches back into the industrial area of the 19th century (cf. Robinson, 2016), and it seems a valid question if similar structures are still the best way forward for today's societies in terms of education as they were conceived more than 100 years ago. Ken Robinson, for example, challenges our industrial model of age grouping and standardisation, among others, in how schools are conceptualised. Similarly, as discussed in the last chapter, earlier voices in the progressive school movement and the de-schooling movement of the 20th century have also called for substantial changes in how (mainstream) schooling can and should look like, often with an eye on the flourishing (even if this term was not used in this way) of students. But are things that different today from how society and life has been 50 or 100 years ago? As so often, the answer is 'yes and no'.

Much in life is the same: one has to work to make a living, one needs food to eat, a place to live and sleep, etc. etc. However, the 'how' of some of these things has indeed changed, and rapidly so over the last 30–40 years. Examples are the development of computers in the 1980s, the advent of the internet in the 1990s, smartphones arrived in the 2000s, and electric and self-driving cars (at least in some places) in the 2010s. In this current decade, we have just seen the emergence of AI (at writing this text, the first Large Language Model AI, ChatGPT, is just about one and a half years old), and the first mass produced humanoid robots marketed for the general population. The reality of work and how many jobs are performed has significantly changed since the beginning of this century, and access to information has become instantaneous and virtually unlimited. It is hard to predict how the latest changes in technology, esp. AI, will impact on people's everyday lives, but AI already has made huge waves in education – as a challenge for assessment, but also as a resource for teachers and students. It seems indicated to ask, and to start thinking about, if holding on to traditional schooling setups of classrooms, standardised assessments, grades, and maybe even schools as the main places of learning, are still the best way forward for our young generation and our societies at large.

Beyond the technological changes in our societies and challenges for schools, we are living (again) in a tumultuous time that sees conflict and war in places we did not expect at the end of the 20th century. The thought that war would happen again in Europe was a distance thought then, but a reality today. In the weeks writing this final chapter in May 2024, the conflict between Israel and Iran has reached a new height of tension and an escalation is not impossible, which could destabilise the whole Middle-Eastern region and potentially lead to further humanitarian crises and mass migration. Since the war in the Ukraine started, hunger in the world has started to rise again for the first time in many years (Von Grebmer et al., 2023). These developments are on top of global warming and the many local crises that come with the increase in global temperature and sea-level rise (e.g., for island nations in the South Pacific). And even in the 'Global North', democracies are under threat, not so much from external but internal ideological challenges through the rise of populist, nationalist and partly fascist movements that seek to undermine the balances of power in some democratic countries. While more could be said about other areas in the world, the list is long enough for us to pose the question of the role of education and schooling in these larger contexts. And, while I do not want to imply that schools and educators can solve these larger societal and global problems, I would argue that education does play a role in equipping each individual to be able to understand and think through some of the complexities involved and consider their own role in the larger picture. This brings us back to an education for the art of living. Being able not just to step into a job that is relevant to the local economy and industry, but to be able to see the interconnections in the world and identify leavers of change is important not just for shaping one's own life actively, but also to be an active and conscientious agent (cf. Biesta, 2022) in the world.

So, what does this mean for teachers and principals today? – I would argue that there is a need for increased tolerance, understanding, flexibility and critical perspectivism (cf. D'Olimpio, 2021) in the world. Students need to develop the hermeneutical skills to interpret and understand the world and what they experience, and they need to develop prudence and practical wisdom to know what the right thing is to do in the situations they find themselves in. As such, incorporating aspects of an art of living education in schools and classrooms can contribute to equipping students with these faculties. However, I would argue that we cannot wait for a large social and political shift, or maybe a revolution of the education system, to happen. As educators, we need to act here and now, and teachers and principals have the power, as curriculum decision makers (cf. McGee, 1997), to act in the sphere of their local contexts. In concrete terms, this can mean to start out on their own journey towards developing their own art of living. Schmid emphasises the importance of engaging in one's own art of living for teachers *of* the art of living. Next, one might want to find like-minded colleagues one can bring on board to create a critical mass of supporters in one's local context. As argued elsewhere (D'Olimpio & Teschers, 2016), creating a whole-school approach in support of people's development of an art of living will be much more effective than individual teachers amending their classroom practice and curriculum. While practices of connecting subject content to the lived reality of students and making content relevant to students' lives, as well as incorporating instances of life-knowledge, as outlined in the previous chapter, can support students' development of their own art of living, a school-wide approach that sees themes across subject areas and takes a deliberate approach to supporting the development of an art of living can certainly be more impactful. This can include a deliberate consideration of how school buildings and grounds are used and presented; how art is used and displayed; how students are included in the creation of art and in the design of the learning environment; how classes are structured, and curriculum is developed. For example, one can ask the question if there is leeway within one's national and local system to offer dedicated art of living classes, or if relevant content can be included in subjects such as ethics or philosophy, English or other languages, social or cultural studies, or whatever is allowed under the current policies in place in the local context. Such whole-school considerations should also not be limited to students, but include the whole school community, including teachers, administrative staff, cleaners, gardeners, the principal, and the wider community. One can further ask how parents can be approached and become interested in their children's art of living – and maybe their own art of living.

Change, however, always comes with difficulties and resistance. As educators concerned about the flourishing and beautiful lives of our students, and maybe also being concerned about the state of our nation and the world, we need to expect and be prepared to face resistance to necessary change. While the topic of how to facilitate change successfully is likely a book in itself written by someone else, a typical reaction we can find in education (and other professions) is the 'we have always done it this way' response, which is one likely contributor to the largely consistent 'grammar of schooling' mentioned above (Tyack & Tobin, 1994). Examples of successful change, I would argue, can help overcome resistance to change. As such, drawing on project schools and progressive education elements that can be shown to have positive effect for students and 'work' for teachers might be helpful. Also, keeping in mind that significant change does not have to be tackled in one go. As Weick (1984) explained, making small wins in local contexts can create a movement that leads to change on a larger scale. As such, making small progress in one's classroom, getting one colleague on board, or sharing relevant information with others might be a small win that contributes to wider change in one's local school or centre environment. Similarly, small wins in various places can over time create a movement towards more structural changes on a national and societal level. Therefore, I want to encourage the interested reader to start on their own journey towards developing their own art of living, pursuing their own beautiful life, and to consider what small wins they could make in their local environment that might contribute to a better future for our children, our society and hopefully our planet.

References

Benade, L. (2017). Is the classroom obsolete in the twenty-first century?. *Educational Philosophy and Theory*, 49(8), 796–807. doi:10.1080/00131857.2016.1269631.

Benade, L. (2019). Flexible learning spaces: Inclusive by design?. *New Zealand Journal of Educational Studies*, 54(1), 53–68. doi:10.1007/s40841-019-00127-2.

Biesta, G. (2022). *World-centred education: A view for the present*. Routledge.

D'Olimpio, L. (2021). Critical perspectivism: Educating for a moral response to media. *Journal of Moral Education*, 50(1), 92–103. doi:10.1080/03057240.2020.1772213.

D'Olimpio, L., & Teschers, C. (2016). 'Philosophy for children meets the art of living: A holistic approach to an education for life. *Philosophical Inquiry in Education*, 23(2), 114–124. doi:10.7202/1070458ar.

Von Grebmer, K. et al. (2023). GLOBAL HUNGER INDEX THE POWER OF YOUTH IN SHAPING FOOD SYSTEMS: A peer-reviewed publication. Available at: www.globalhungerindex.org (Accessed: 2 May 2024).

McGee, Clive. (1997). *Teachers and curriculum decision-making*. Dunmore Press.

Patrix, M., & Benade, L. (2018). *Beyond the building. Reconceptualising learning environments: A literature review, New Zealand Journal of Teachers' Work*.

Robinson, K. (2016). *Creative schools*. Penguin.

Tyack, D., & Tobin, W. (1994). The "Grammar" of schooling: Why has it been so hard to change?. *American Educational Research Journal*, 31(3), 453–479. doi:10.3102/00028312031003453.

Weick, K. E. (1984). Small wins – Redefining the scale of social problems. *American Psychologist*, 39(1), 40–49.

CREDITS

The author and publisher gratefully acknowledge permission to reproduce material from the following sources.

Chapter Two and parts of Chapter Three incorporate material, with permission, from a previous book chapter 'Education towards a beautiful life in an imperfect world', published by Peter Lang in Kamp et al. (Eds.), 2023, *Wellbeing – Global Policies and Perspectives. Insights from Aotearoa New Zealand and beyond.*

Chapter Three is informed by and contains substantial material in edited form, with permission, from work previously published in the Journal of the Canadian Philosophy of Education Society *Philosophical Inquiry in Education*: Teschers, C., & Nieto, M. (2023). Buen Vivir and the art of living: Comparing Western and Latin American perspectives on living a 'good life'. *PIE*, 30(3), 207–220.

INDEX

adequacy in education 64
agency 34, 45, 110
aims in education 82
Ainscow 60
Aotearoa. New Zealand
Aristotle 9, 16–17, 19, 21, 32, 92
art of living 7–8, 20–22, 37, 44, 48, 70, 79
   definition 89
   develop 73
   environment 48
   faculties 10–11, 25, 51, 93, 106–107, 120
   for good of society 51
authentic 22
Autio, T. 97, 109

Ballard, K. 59
beautiful life 7, 20, 26, 33, 42, 71, 92–93
becoming of *a* self 84
beliefs 2, 8–9, 11, 17, 21–23, 27–28, 33, 35, 37, 39–40, 47–50, 66, 70, 72–73, 85, 87, 90–91, 101–102
Bevan-Brown, J. 59

Bieri, P. 34
Biesta, G. 4, 80, 83
Bildung 11, 73, 80, 86, 98, 100
bottomless pit problem 65
Bourdieu, P. 11
Bowles and Gintis 59, 63
Brighouse, H. 59
buen vivir 38, 40–41

Challenges for people's life 1
change
   in education 117
   difficulties 121
   world 119
Coleman, J.S. 59, 63, 69
Communities of (philosophical) Inquiry (CoI) 106
community good 47
community wellbeing 22, 41
compassion 67
Competency-based learning 98
complexities of life 3

INDEX

Csikszentmihalyi, M. 71
currere 104
curriculum 26, 102, 104, 110
  knowledge areas 26, 74, 78
  knowledge themes. knowledge areas

D'Olimpio, L. 106
de-schooling movement 111
despair 33
Dewey, J. 73, 79, 111

educated subject 101–102, 104
education
  competencies 97–98
  end of 82
  for the art of living 10, 24, 51, 97
  understanding of 65, 80
education systems. schooling
enlightened self-interest 9, 23, 35, 36, 40
Entfaltung 80
Epicurus 32
equal educational opportunity 52, 59, 63, 68
equality 61
  in education 63
equity 51–52, 59, 63, 71, 112
Erziehung 80, 100
ethics 35
  art of living 9, 21, 31, 35, 37, 40, 47, 85
ethics of care. ethics:art of living
ethics of practical wisdom. ethics:art of living
eudaimonia 16, 21, 32, 88
evaluation
  of education systems 110

fairness. equity
Feldman, F. 7
Finish education system 87, 99, 109
flourishing 16, 19, 87
  pre-conditions 92
Foucault, M. 36
freedom 50

good education 17, 84, 117
good life 7, 31, 34, 39, 42

Gosepath, S. 61
grammar of schooling 111
happiness 71
  serene 16
  utmost 16

hedonic 18–19, 32
hermeneutical process 103
holistic
  education 81–82, 97–102, 104
  life 26, 53, 71, 101
  wellbeing 15, 19–20, 28
Human flourishing. *flourishing*

Indigenous. *Worldviews:indigenous*
interconnections in the world 11, 22, 44, 86

justice. equity

Kowii, A. 38
Kristjánsson, K. 17, 88

Lam, C. 23
learnification 83, 98
Lederer, B. 100
Liebau, E. 81
life-knowledge 10–103
life-satisfaction 16, 71
limitations of current education
  systems 112

MacIntyre, A. 88
meaning of life 92
Millett and Tapper 106
Montessori, M. 111
Müller-Commichau, W. 19

Neill, A.S. 111
neoliberal. neoliberal ideology
neoliberal ideology 4, 8, 25, 51, 70
neoliberalism. neoliberal ideology
New Zealand context 3–6, 23, 25, 36, 38, 44, 54, 98, 108, 117

norms. *beliefs*
Nussbaum and Sen 73

Paradox of Choice 2
pedagogy 26, 102, 106–108, 110
Peters, R. S. 79
Peterson, A. 67
Philosophy 103, 107
Philosophy for Children (P4C) 106
phronésis 9–10, 21, 23, 35, 39, 43, 90, 105, 110
Pinar, W. 103
positive education 18, 88
positive psychology 16, 88
　critique 19
Prage, L. 38
progressive school movement 111
prudence and practical wisdom. *phronésis*
purposes of education 80

qualification 86

Rawls, J. 62
reconceptualisation of schooling 111
relevance of schooling 26
Roberts, P. 33
Robinson, K. 118

Satz, D. 63
Schmid, W. 7, 23, 27, 33, 35
schooling 28, 53, 63, 66, 68, 71, 84, 98, 109
　aims of 79–80
　education vs training 81

　inclusive 100–101
　outcome of 68
　reform vs. revolution 109
　relation to education 80
Schwartz, B. 2
self-reflection 37, 47
Seligma, M. 16–17, 19
serene happiness. *happiness:serene*
Socialisation 86
Steiner, R. 111
student wellbeing 17
subjectification 18, 34, 84
subjective wellbeing 16

te ao Māori. *worldviews:Māori*
teachers
　implications for 120
tolerance 48
Tortosa, J.M. 38

values. *beliefs*
wellbeing 15, 24
　holistic approach 20
　limited focus 16
　range of definitions 16

White, J. 63
whole-school approach 120
world-centred education 83, 85
worldviews 3, 36–37
　indigenous 3, 6, 99–100
　Māori 5, 44
　Western 3

COMPLICATED
A BOOK SERIES OF CURRICULUM STUDIES

Reframing the curricular challenge educators face after a decade of school deform, the books published in Peter Lang's Complicated Conversation Series testify to the ethical demands of our time, our place, our pro- fession. What does it mean for us to teach now, in an era structured by political polarization, economic destabi- lization, and the prospect of climate catastrophe? Each of the books in the Complicated Conversation Series provides provocative paths, theoretical and practical, to a very different future. In this resounding series of scholarly and pedagogical inter- ventions into the night- mare that is the present, we hear once again the sound of silence breaking, supporting us to rearticulate our pedagogical convictions in this time of terrorism, reframing curriculum as committed to the com- plicated conversation that is intercultural communication, self-understanding, and global justice.

The series editor is

> Dr. William F. Pinar
> Department of Curriculum Studies
> 2125 Main Mall
> Faculty of Education
> University of British Columbia
> Vancouver, British Columbia V6T 1Z4
> CANADA

To order other books in this series, please contact our Customer Service Department:

> peterlang@presswarehouse.com (within the U.S.)
> orders@peterlang.com (outside the U.S.)

Or browse online by series:

> www.peterlang.com

www.ingramcontent.com/pod-product-compliance
Lightning Source LLC
Chambersburg PA
CBHW061719300426
44115CB00014B/2749